CAPTAIN JACK'S BASIC NAVIGATION

JACK I. DAVIS

Editor: John P. Kaufman
Copy Editor: John P. O'Connor, Jr.

BRISTOL FASHION PUBLICATIONS, INC.
Harrisburg, Pennsylvania

Captain Jack's Basic Navigation, By Jack I. Davis

Published by Bristol Fashion Publications, Inc.

Copyright © 1998 by Jack I. Davis. All rights reserved.

No part of this book may be reproduced or used in any form or by any means-graphic, electronic, mechanical, including photocopying, recording, taping or information storage and retrieval systems-without written permission of the publisher.

BRISTOL FASHION PUBLICATIONS AND THE AUTHOR HAVE MADE EVERY EFFORT TO INSURE THE ACCURACY OF THE INFORMATION PROVIDED IN THIS BOOK BUT ASSUMES NO LIABILITY WHATSOEVER FOR SAID INFORMATION OR THE CONSEQUENCES OF USING THE INFORMATION PROVIDED IN THIS BOOK.

ISBN: 1-892216-09-4
LCCN: 98-074176

Contribution acknowledgments

Cover Art and inside illustrations by Joe Kolb, unless otherwise indicated.

Captain Jack's Basic Navigation, By Jack I. Davis

INTRODUCTION

I have about 30,000 blue water sailing miles behind me plus another 5,000 blue water power boat miles. Add to that 5,000 very boring Intracoastal waterway miles and some 1,000 three or four hour sailing lessons and you can see I've spent a lot of time on boats. Most of this time has been thoroughly enjoyable.

Some of the less joyful things are storms. Storms at sea are not much fun and storms lasting for weeks at a time are not much fun for weeks at a time. We have to take the bad with the good.

When I first started to teach sailing courses, I was surprised at the satisfaction I derived from the experience. For me, there is a sense of accomplishment which didn't exist in many of my other endeavors.

After going through the basics of sailing, many of my sailing students wanted to further improve their knowledge of the sea. This led me into teaching my first navigation classes.

Teaching these navigation classes was satisfying, but frustration began when I could not get through to many of the students. I learned that most of these slow students weren't slow at all. They just had an inept instructor. ME!

By refining my techniques and borrowing ideas from others, I found I had fewer and fewer slow students. This book utilizes the same techniques as a method for the reader to become a competent navigator.

The format presented here is the classroom presentation.

Captain Jack's Basic Navigation, By Jack I. Davis

Included is my practice of interspersing many of my sea stories with the real work. Of course, these are the same stories my former students are already more familiar with than they want to be.

Many of my explanations, diagrams and procedures have come about as the most practical way for me to introduce newcomers to the navigational procedures on a boat. They may not reflect absolute scientific explanation but they will teach you what you must know.

I must admit, I've picked up many ideas and techniques from others. Too numerous to mention them all but I do want to acknowledge a few of the main ones.

First, many years ago I took an Intermediate Navigation correspondence course from the University of Tennessee. This was my first and only venture into the academic aspects of navigation. It was a good venture, and in reviewing my teaching methods, I see the influence of that well-structured course.

Second, in preparing for my first U. S. Coast Guard captain's license examination, I reviewed a book by Richard A. Block, published by Marine Education Textbooks. His navigation presentation was by far the best and most comprehensive of any on the market. I know my teaching methods have been greatly affected by Mr. Block's work.

Third, the number one authority on navigation, in my opinion, is Bowditch. I use both Volumes I and II extensively.

Last but not least, I must acknowledge and thank the hundreds of sailors I have sailed with through the years. I have learned something, from nearly every one of them, which influences my teaching and definitely my sea stories.

I want to especially thank Lynn Pinkerton and Sandy Billings for encouraging me to write this book and my first mate, Mary, for spelling and grammar lessons I somehow missed in school. Joe Kolb for artwork and friendship. Mike Sutton my sailboat neighbor, who worked the problems and checked the answers.

Jack I. Davis

Captain Jack's Basic Navigation, By Jack I. Davis

Captain Jack's Basic Navigation, By Jack I. Davis

Captain Jack's Basic Navigation, By Jack I. Davis

TABLE OF CONTENTS

Introduction — Page 5

Chapter 1 *Distance, Speed and Time* — Page 15

Distance, Speed and Time Answers — Page 25

Chapter 2 *Learn to Sail* — Page 27

Chapter 3 *Compass* — Page 29

Compass Answers — Page 43

Chapter 4 *To Be A Better Sailor* — Page 47

Chapter 5 *Distance of the Horizon* — Page 51

Distance of the Horizon Answers — Page 57

Chapter 6 *Heavy Weather Sailing* — Page 59

Chapter 7 *Bow & Beam Bearings* — Page 65

Bow & Beam Bearings Answers — Page 71

Captain Jack's Basic Navigation, By Jack I. Davis

Chapter 8 *Learn to Maneuver Your Boat* — Page 79

Chapter 9 *Chart Reading* — Page 81

Chapter 10 *Plotting* — Page 85

    Plotting Answers — Page 97

Chapter 11 *Follow Your Navigational Plan* — Page 101

Chapter 12 *Fear, Remembrance and Reality* — Page 103

Sailing Terms Spoken Every Day — Page 109

Suppliers and Manufacturers — Page 111

Glossary — Page 115

About The Author — Page 131

Captain Jack's Basic Navigation, By Jack I. Davis

Captain Jack's Basic Navigation, By Jack I. Davis

Captain Jack's Basic Navigation, By Jack I. Davis

Figure 1

Captain Jack's Basic Navigation, By Jack I. Davis

Figure 2

Chapter 1
DISTANCE SPEED AND TIME

Being a good navigator can't be traced to one single skill. It's a composite of many talents.

Today, with the availability of electronic aids, such as GPS (Global Positioning System), you could cross an ocean without the navigational talents in this book. Provided there is no electronic failure.

I see inexperienced people go to sea without the proper abilities. Many make their landfall without major problems but there are some who do have complications. I talked to one of these people and his comment was, "When the electronics failed, it was the most frightening experience of my life. I was not only lost, but I didn't even know where I was before I was lost."

Which brings us to:

Figure 3

Captain Jack's Basic Navigation, By Jack I. Davis

Rule # 1 - Always maintain a D. R.

These letters stand for *Dead Reckoning*. All the time you are under way, keep a record of the course, speed and the elapsed time.

I can not overemphasize the importance of keeping a systematic record of your distance, speed and elapsed time, while at sea. For the electronic sailor who does not maintain a DR, I recommended he glue a mirror just below his GPS or Loran. When the electronics fail, he can then look in the mirror and see who is lost.

In order to plot your course, time and speed onto your chart, you must learn to calculate distance, speed and time.

Don't worry about the difficult calculations. The most complicated math involved in our navigational procedures is elementary math. As simple as it is, you should use your hand held calculator to further simplify checking the answers.

Everyone does a certain amount of these calculations while driving from point A to point B. If these points are 60 miles apart and your car speed is 60 miles per hour, it's going to take an hour to make the trip. You can conclude: You're traveling one mile per minute at 60 miles per hour, in 30 minutes you will be halfway there. Navigation is that simple.

In this case you are solving for distance. You know your speed (60 mph) and the elapsed time (30 minutes). The formula to solve this problem is D̲istance = S̲peed x T̲ime. We put down 60 mph for speed and .5 for elapsed time (30 minutes is one half of an hour, or .5). Then 60 times .5 equals 30, or 30 miles, the answer to the problem.

We may also need to solve for speed. This formula is:

S = D / T (The / symbol represents *Divided By*). If we have made 30 miles in 30 minutes (.5 hours) we divide 30 by .5 which equals 60 (mph).

To solve for time, the formula is T = D / S. If we have traveled 30 miles at a speed of 60 mph, we divide the 30 by 60 which equals .5 (.5 hr = 30 minutes)

These formulae are critical. If you use the wrong formula,

as is so easy to do, the answer will definitely be wrong. Instead of trying to remember all these formulas there is a better solution.

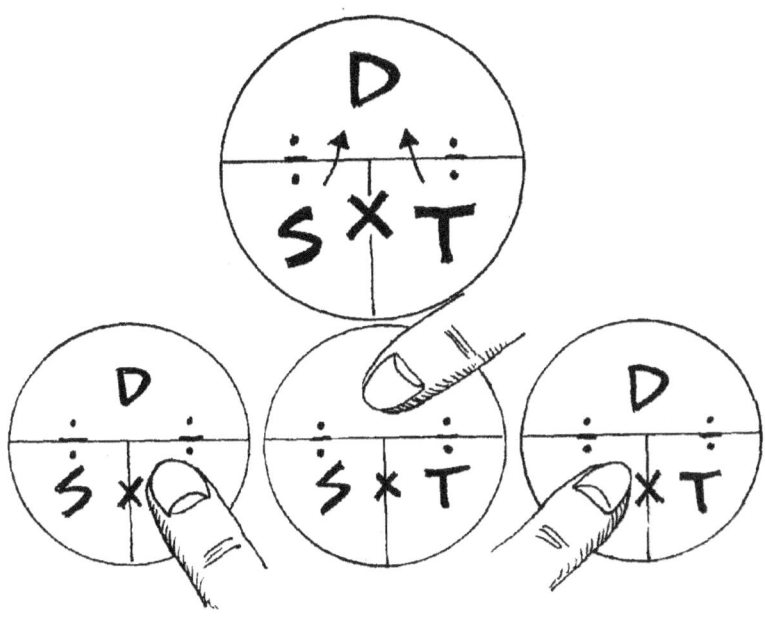

Figure 4

This figure includes all three formulas: To solve for T (time) you divide D by S. To Solve for D (distance) you multiply S times T. To solve for S (speed) you divide D by T.

Please be certain you understand this and do not try to remember the formulas. Always write the formula on the work paper.

In the examples given for distance, speed and time, the examples were mph (miles per hour) and the distances were statue miles, used by most landlubbers. The statue mile is 5,280 feet, but the nautical mile is 6,080 feet.

Everything shown from here on will be nautical miles (nm) and knots (kn). Note, I did not say knots per hour, which is incorrect.

Captain Jack's Basic Navigation, By Jack I. Davis

A knot is the speed of 1 nautical mile per hour. Derived from the Common Log where the number of knots (about 25 feet apart) which ran out in a quarter minute gave a direct reading of the ship's speed. Thus, if the log was streamed and six knots ran out before the quarter-minute glass ran out, the ship's speed was six knots. To say 6 knots per hour is, strictly speaking, incorrect.

I use the abbreviation *hr* for hours and *min* for minutes. Remember: when you multiply or divide hours and minutes, you must convert your minutes to fractions of an hour. For instance: 2 hr 15 min must be converted to 2.25 hr (divide your minutes by 60). 15/60 minutes equals .25 hr.

When you have found an answer that is hours and fractions of hours, you must convert it back: 2.25 hr must be converted to 2 hr 15 min (You multiply the fraction by 60). .25 X 60 equals 15 min.

If I am using a hand held calculator, I carry all the decimal places that the gadget will allow me to carry: 2 hr 22 min (22/60 equals .36666666).

If I must use long division or multiplication (with paper and pencil), I round off to .367. The difference will be acceptable.

It is important to work all of the following problems, even if you think you know how to do them. You may be surprised. The answers are at the end of this chapter.

DISTANCE	SPEED	TIME
1. _____ ?	7 kn	3 hr
2. _____ ?	5.5 kn	4 hr
3. _____ ?	13.5 kn	3.5 hr
4. _____ ?	17 kn	3 hr 10 min
5. _____ ?	24 kn	3 hr 10 min

Captain Jack's Basic Navigation, By Jack I. Davis

6. _____? 2.7 kn .8 hr

7. _____? 42.4 kn 16 min

8. _____? 23 kn 46 min

9. 43 nm 6.2 kn _____?

10. 32 nm 8.5 kn _____?

11. 35 nm 12.3 kn _____?

12. 17 nm 28 kn _____?

13. 15 nm 3.5 kn _____?

14. 17.8 nm 29 kn _____?

15. 6.6 nm 19.3 kn _____?

16. 8.1 nm 16.9 kn _____?

17. 22 nm _____? 29 min

18. 23.8 nm _____? 0.6 hr

19. 12.3 nm _____? 19 min

20. 34 nm _____? 88 min

21. 24.1 nm _____? 77 min

22. 16.5 nm _____? 0.48 hr

23. 18.9 nm _____? 0.77 hr

24. 17.1 nm _____? 1.5 hr

Captain Jack's Basic Navigation, By Jack I. Davis

In school, the stated problem was one of my least favorite problems. Life, as it turns out, is a stated problem. Certainly, navigation on a small boat is a stated problem. Don't be intimidated. Try to look at each problem as if it is a real life situation and you are the navigator in charge.

25. The distance between two buoys is 14 nm. The vessel's speed is 11 kn. The running time between the two buoys is _____?

26. Your boat's speed is 12 kn. The speed of the current is 3 kn. What is the speed of your boat over the bottom while going upstream against the current _____?

27. Your boat's speed is 12 kn. The current's drift is 2 kn. (The speed of a current is called drift). What is the speed of your boat over the bottom as it travels downstream with the current _____?

28. If you have a 2 kn current and can make 13 kn with a 6 nm run in each direction, how long would it take for a round trip _____?

Be certain to work this problem as two separate legs then add the results together. The answer will surprise most folks.

29. Point "B" is 59 nm from point "A" on a course of 345 degrees true. The current sets 165 degrees true at a drift of 1.7 kn. If your vessel's speed is 12.6 kn, how long will it take you to reach point "B" from point "A"_____?

You already know drift is the speed of the current. Now, here is a new term: Set. Set is the direction the current is going.

30. Your course from "B" to "A" is north on a leg of 10 nm. Your boat's speed is 10 kn. The current's set is 180

degrees with a drift of 4 kn. What is your speed over the bottom _____?

31. Your vessel is making way through the water at a speed of 13 kn. Your vessel traveled 30 nm in 4 hr 23 min. What current are you experiencing _____?

Captain Jack's Basic Navigation, By Jack I. Davis

Figure 5, 6 and 7

Captain Jack's Basic Navigation, By Jack I. Davis

DISTANCE SPEED TIME ANSWERS

1. 7 kn x 3 hr = 21 nm

2. 5.5 kn x 4 hr = 22 nm

3. 13.5 kn x 3.5 hr = 47.25 nm

4. 17 kn x 3.1666666 = 53.8333 nm

5. 24 kn x 3.16666 hr = 75.9 nm

6. 2.7 kn x .8 hr = 2.16 nm

7. 42.4 kn x .266666 hr = 11.30666 nm

8. 23 kn x .7666666 = 17.6333 nm

9. 43 nm / 6.2 kn = 6.9354838 hr or 6:56 hr & min

10. 32 nm / 8.5 kn = 3.7647058 hr or 3:46 hr & min

11. 35 nm / 12.3 kn = 2.8455284 hr or 2:51 hr & min

12. 17 nm / 28 kn = .6071428 hr or 0:36 min

13. 15 nm / 3.5 kn = 4.2857142 hr or 4:17 hr & min

Captain Jack's Basic Navigation, By Jack I. Davis

14. 17.8 nm / 29 kn = .613793 hr or 0:37 min

15. 6.6 nm / 19.3 kn = .341968 hr or 0:21 min

16. 8.1 nm / 16.9 kn = .4792899 hr or 0:29 min

17. 22 nm / .483333 hr = 45.517 kn

18. 23.8 nm / .6 hr = 39.666 kn

19. 12.3 nm / .316666 hr = 38.842 kn

20. 34 nm / 1.4666666 hr = 23.1818 kn

21. 24.1 nm / 1.2833 hr = 18.779 kn

22. 16.5 nm / 0.48 hr = 34.375 kn

23. 18.9 / .77 hr = 24.545 kn

24. 17.1 nm / 1.5 hr = 11.4 kn

25. 14 nm / 11 kn = 1:16 hr & min

26. 12 kn - 3 kn = 9 kn

27. 12 kn + 2 kn = 14 kn

28. Work as two legs:
    1st leg 6 nm - (13 - 2) =   .54545
    2nd leg 6 nm - (13 + 2) =   .40000
                                   .94545 hr

The temptation in this problem is to reason that the current coming and going balances out. Therefore, you could simply use 13 kn = 0:55384 min which will not provide the correct answer.

29. Then:
   59 nm / 10.9 kn = 5.41284 hr
   Then:
   .41284 X 60 = :247706 min = 5 hr 25 min

30. The course - North (360 degrees)
    The current sets South (180 degrees)
    Speed 6 kn

31. 30 nm - 4.383333 hr = 6.844111 kn (Speed made good)   Then:
    Boat speed 13 kn
    less 6.8441111 (speed made good)
    drift 6.155889 (speed of current)

Captain Jack's Basic Navigation, By Jack I. Davis

Chapter 2
LEARN TO SAIL

When I bought my first sailboat, the owner went with me on a sea trial which lasted about three hours. That was the extent of my formal sailing education. The balance came in the most difficult way possible, trial and error. In retrospect, it was as much a comedy of errors as a learning experience. I cringe to think of the daily horror stories my little boat and I lived through.

It would have been far better to pay someone to teach me properly, than to get myself beat up so many times. My survival is a true tribute to the strength and integrity of my boat.

Reading the sailing stories of others and their mistakes helped me avoid a few of my own but the better choice would have been lessons.

There are hundreds of charter operators in the nation who offer these lessons and the charge for the course will be money well spent. Of course, some are better than others. Ask for references and check them out carefully before spending your hard-earned money.

There are also Learn to Sail schools and sailing vacation charters with sailing lessons thrown in. I don't like this approach as they seem to throw a lot at their students in a short period of time. Several of my sailing students had been through a concentrated six-day school. They knew less than the students who had been through five lessons of four hours each. The less concentrated course provided the time in between the lessons to absorb the experience.

There are a few sailing school operators who take students out on pleasure cruises. There are refreshments, congeniality and camaraderie, but they impart very little sailing knowledge. I find nothing wrong with people going out to have fun, but I resent those operators referring to their operations as schools.

In most Learn to Sail programs, the student is exposed to different boats and the more the better. You must know the good and the bad attributes of boats before you start on the boat buying trail.

Between the upcoming navigation chapters, there will be further advice and recommendations for the sailors who intend to pursue the cruising life.

Chapter 3
COMPASS

If you draw a line from where you are standing to the North Pole, that direction would be true north. A magnetic compass does not point toward the North Pole, instead it points toward magnetic north.

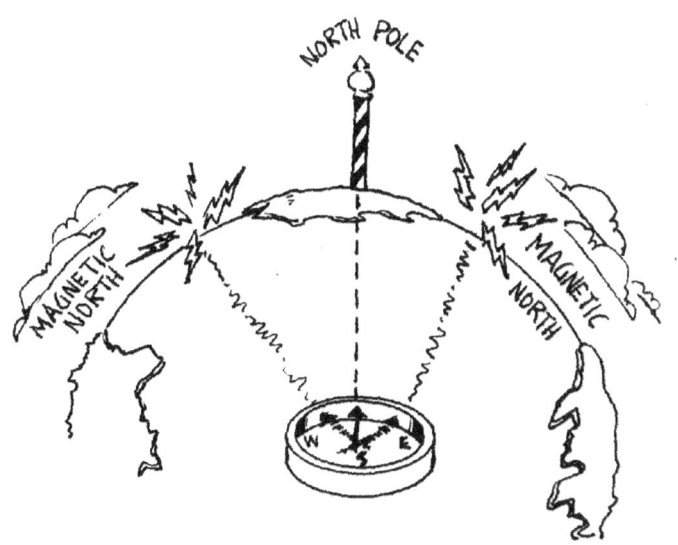

Figure 9

Captain Jack's Basic Navigation, By Jack I. Davis

Magnetic north is fairly close to the North Pole but far enough away to cause some major differences. Because of the earth's magnetic pattern, this magnetic north position changes from area to area. This difference between true north and magnetic north is called variation.

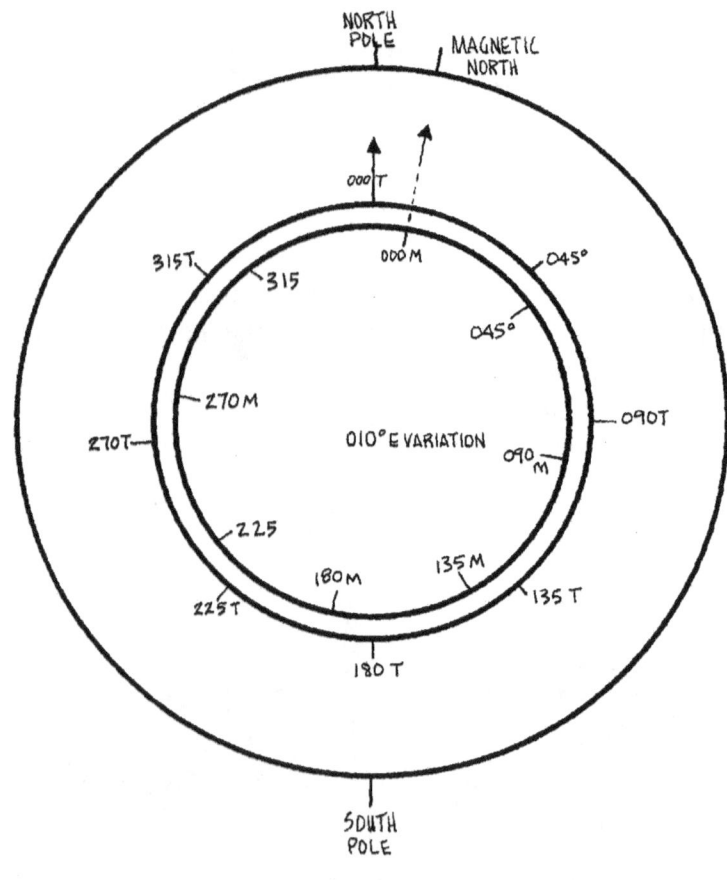

Figure 8

The outer compass rose points toward the North Pole.

When Columbus left the Mediterranean on his expedition to find a shorter route to the far east, he was only familiar with the zero magnetic variation that exists in much of the area between Spain and Italy. The Mediterranean sailors of that time checked their compass against Polaris, the North Star.

The captains and crews of that expedition were shocked to find the farther west they went in the Atlantic, the more their compasses were off in relation to Polaris. We know now that in the mid-Atlantic, the compass variation was as much as twenty degrees, and then it slowly decreases as you move further west. When Columbus made landfall in the Bahamas, the variation was down to two degrees.

All of the charts we use for navigation show the compass variation. This must be taken into consideration in our plotting.

Each of these charts has a compass rose in one or more places on the chart. See figure 8. The compass rose is made up of two parts:

The outer rose, which points toward true north.

The inner rose, which points to magnetic north for that area of the chart.

In the center of the rose the amount of variation and whether the variation is east or west is shown, along with the rate of annual change. This annual change is a very small number and if the charts are fairly recent, the change is of little importance. With very old charts, however, the accumulated annual changes could add up and be a concern, but then again, you shouldn't be using very old charts.

In addition to variation, another situation can affect your ship's compass. All metal on board, either magnetic or nonmagnetic, can move the compass needle. This movement is called deviation.

Deviation on a vessel does not necessarily remain constant. If you move a radio from one location to another, the deviation can change dramatically. This is caused by the magnets used in the construction of the speakers. Occasionally, even canned goods may have an effect, if you put them on board close to the compass.

I spent an hour swinging the compass on a new boat I was to deliver from St. Petersburg to Houston. Later, I noticed a soda can hidden close behind the compass. When I moved it, the compass needle moved fifteen degrees. I then started over and spent another hour swinging the compass.

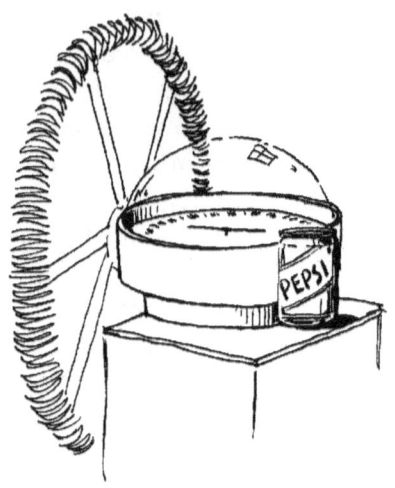

Figure 10

Deviation Card					
Compass	Deviation	Compass	Deviation	Compass	Deviation
000°	001° E	123.7°	005° W	225°	003° W
011.2°	002° E	135°	006° W	236.2°	002° W
022.5°	002° E	146.2°	006° W	247.5°	002° W
033.8°	001° E	157.5°	004° W	258.7°	002° W
045°	001° E	168.7°	004° W	270°	002° W
056.2°	000°	180°	004° W	281.2°	001° W
067.5°	000°	191.2°	003° W	292.5°	001° W
078.8°	002° W	202.5°	003° W	303.7°	000°
090°	003° W	213.7°	003° W	315°	000°
101.2°	004° W	225°	003° W	236.2°	000°
112.5°	005° W	236.2°	003° W	337.5°	001° W
				348.7°	001° W

Table 1 JID

A typical deviation card

Captain Jack's Basic Navigation, By Jack I. Davis

You can have your compass swung, by a professional to determine the deviation, or you can learn to do this yourself. In any event, you will then have a deviation card showing the amount of deviation on several headings.

Next, we will present some basic procedures for checking deviation so you can pick up changes which may occur.

With variation and deviation we must have a system, first of all, for correcting the compass:

While sailing let's assume our compass reads 234°
On that heading, our deviation card shows +005° E
We add the east correction giving us 239°
Our chart shows a variation of +005° E
We add the east correction giving us 244°
The true course we plot on our chart would be 244°

How can you remember when to add and when to subtract? There is a memory guide for this system as follows:

Compass - we substitute the C in compass   Can
Deviation - we substitute the D in deviation   Dead
Magnetic - we substitute the M in magnetic   Men
Variation - we substitute the V in variation   Vote
True - we substitute the T in true   Twice

You can remember "Can dead men vote twice" and add to that AT ELECTION, a reminder to ADD EAST

Many navigators only learn this one system and when they are un-correcting they simply reverse the above procedure, but that can be confusing for most of us. My recommendation is using this un-correcting memory guide:

True - we substitute the T in true   True
Variation - we substitute the V in variation   Virgins
Magnetic - we substitute the M in magnetic   Make
Deviation - we substitute the D in deviation   Dull
Compass - we substitute the C in compass   Companions

Captain Jack's Basic Navigation, By Jack I. Davis

We can remember "True virgins make dull companions" and we add to that ADD WHISKEY, to remind us to ADD WEST.

When I sit down at the chart table to plot courses, I put both of these reminders in one corner of my work papers, and the D-S-T symbol in the other. Most of the experienced navigators I've met do the same. It would be risky to work navigation problems off the top of your head.

The following are navigation problems in which you will use your newly learned talents. We will be introducing some words and phrases you will need, so be certain to work all the problems.

You desire to make good a course of 090° True. The variation taken from the nearest compass rose on your chart is 005° E. The deviation shown for an easterly heading on your boat's deviation card is 010° W. What course will you steer _____?

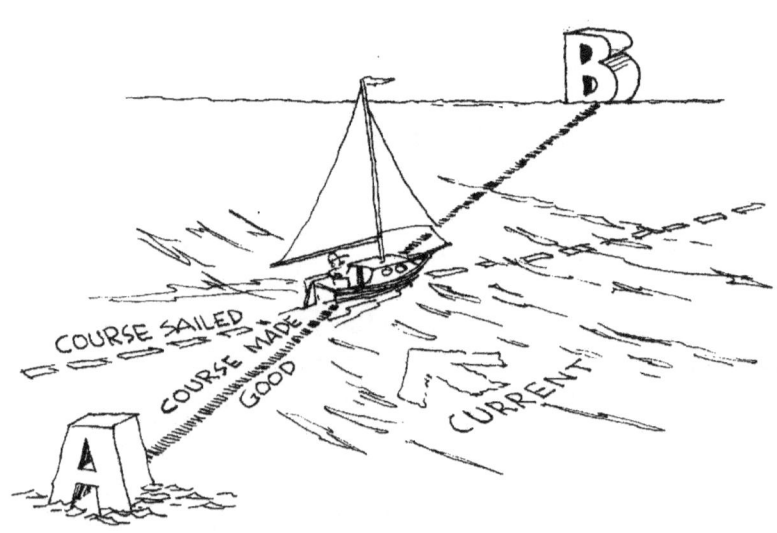

Figure 11

The "Course Made Good" shown in figure 11, is what you want to accomplish. There may be a strong current, variation and deviation. The true course from point A to point B is 090°, but you must steer 075° to get there. When you arrive you have made good a course of 090°.

2. The true course you want to make good, as taken from the chart, is 304 . The deviation on this heading is 006° E and the variation is 013° W. What is the compass course you would steer _____?

3. The true course you want to make good is 276°. The chart shows the variation in your locality is 012° E. The deviation for this heading is 004° W. What is the compass course to steer _____?

Many of the errors during these correcting procedures are caused by not lining up the numbers correctly. The neater, the better.

T	333°
V	002° W
M	335° (Always use three digits)
D	+ 003° E
C	332°

4.
Course	310° T
Deviation	005° E
Variation	015° W
Compass course	_____ ?

5.
Course	135° T
Deviation	002° E
Variation	015° W
Compass course	_____ ?

6. Course   135° T
    Deviation   006° W
    Variation   012° W
    Compass course   _____?

7. Course   020° T
    Deviation   002° E
    Variation   005° W
    Compass course   _____?

8. Course   075° T
    Deviation   002° W
    Variation   029° E
    Compass course   _____?

9. Course   055° T
    Deviation   007° E
    Variation   014° W
    Compass course   _____?

10. Course   150° T
    Deviation   002° E
    Variation   023° W
    Compass course   _____?

11. Course   104° T
    Deviation   002° E
    Variation   010° W
    Compass course   _____?

12. Course   080° T
    Deviation   003° W
    Variation   022° E
    Compass course   _____?

13. Course   021° T
    Deviation   009° W
    Variation   012° W
    Compass course _____?

14. Course   060° T
    Deviation   006° E
    Variation   011° W
    Compass course _____?

15. Course   323° T
    Deviation   006° E
    Variation   012° W
    Compass course _____?

16. Course   175° T
    Deviation   002° W
    Variation   021° W
    Compass course _____?

17. A range is known to be 111° true. You have the ranges in line and directly over the stern. The variation shown on the compass rose is 006°.5` W. If your compass has no deviation, the compass heading should be _____?

18. A vessel is heading 270° PSC. On this heading the deviation is 004° W. The variation is 012° E. The true heading is _____? PSC (Per Ship's Compass)

19. A lighthouse bears 237° PSC. Variation is 014° W. Deviation is 001° E. What is the true bearing of the lighthouse _____?

Bearing - The direction from your ship to an object. The bearing of an object is not related to your heading. The bearings of different objects will become increasingly important as we continue.

Captain Jack's Basic Navigation, By Jack I. Davis

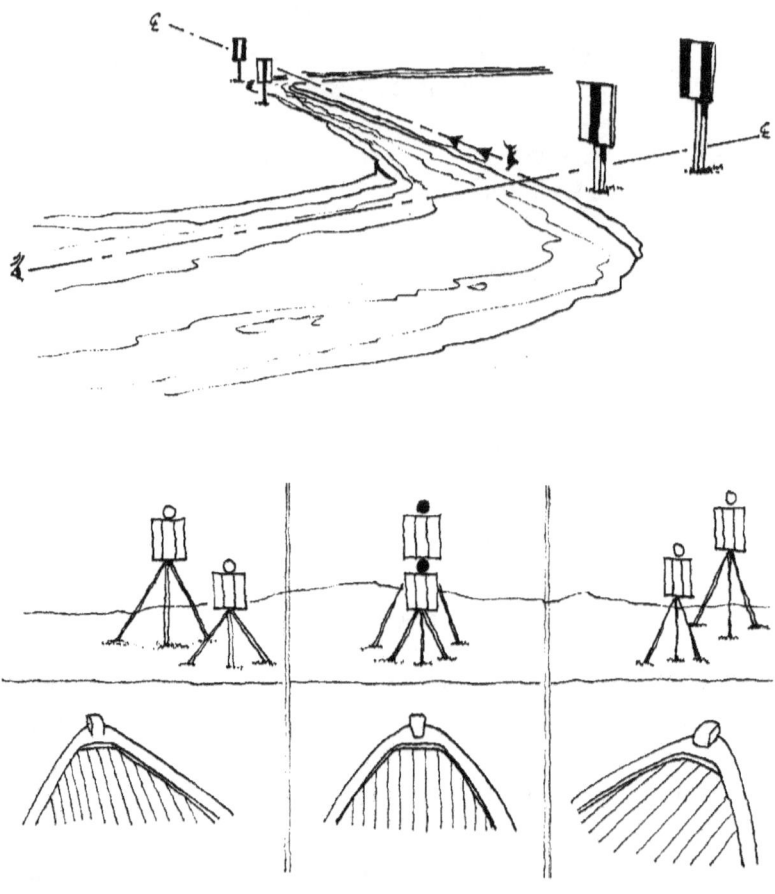

Figure 12

Range markers are used along deep water channels at the bends and turns to give traffic a visual impression of the center of the channel. Looking down the channel, the first range marker you see might be twenty feet tall. The next marker, in line, might be sixty feet tall and one-half mile further down the channel. When you are approaching these markers and have them lined up one above the other, you are precisely in the middle of the channel.

20. PSC 155°
    Deviation 004° E
    Variation 008° W
    _____?

21. PSC 168°
    Deviation 006° W
    Variation 008° W
    _____?

22. PSC 076°
    Deviation 000°
    Variation 005° W
    _____?

23. PSC 153°
    Deviation 003° W
    Variation 012° E
    _____?

24. PSC 228°
    Deviation 003° E
    Variation 023° E
    _____?

25. PSC 120°
    Deviation 002°.5` E
    Variation 022°.5` E
    _____?

26. PSC 071°
    Deviation 006° E
    Variation 002° W
    _____?

27.	PSC 034°
	Deviation 010° W
	Variation 020° W
	_____?

28.	PSC 081°
	Deviation 010° W
	Variation 019° E
	_____?

29. The bearing of a range taken from the inner circle of the compass rose on a local chart was found to be 177°. The bearing of the same range taken on the boat's compass was 175°. What was the deviation of the compass on that particular boat. _____?

30. Two range lights are in line bearing 054° by compass. The true direction of the range is 049°. Variation according to the chart is 010° W. The deviation of the compass is _____?

31. The deviation of a compass for a 235° compass reading and 232° true course with a variation of 004° E is _____?

32. Three buoys in line bear 062° by the magnetic compass rose on a chart. When parallel with these buoys, your compass reads 058°. What is your deviation on this heading _____?

33.	Magnetic 200°
	Compass 178°
	Deviation
	_____?

34. PSC 091°
    True 084°
    Variation 008° W
    Deviation _____ ?

35. PSC 015°
    True 010°
    Variation 021° E
    Deviation _____ ?

36. A set of ranges is known to be 344° true. You have these ranges in line directly off your beam. The variation shown on your chart is 007°.25` W. If your compass heading is 264°.25`, your deviation should be _____ ?

37. True course 000°
    Deviation 007° E
    Variation 012° W
    PSC _____ ?

38. True course 360°
    Deviation 016° E
    Variation 016° E
    PSC _____ ?

Captain Jack's Basic Navigation, By Jack I. Davis

Captain Jack's Basic Navigation, By Jack I. Davis

COMPASS ANSWERS

1	2	3	4	5
T $090°$	T $304°$	T $276°$	T $310°$	T $135°$
V $005°$ E	V $013°$ W	V $012°$ E	V $015°$ W	V $015°$ W
M $085°$	M $317°$	M $264°$	M $325°$	M $150°$
D $010°$ W	D $006°$ E	D $004°$ W	D $005°$ E	D $002°$ E
C $095°$	C $311°$	C $268°$	C $320°$	C $148°$

6	7	8	9	10
T $135°$	T $020°$	T $075°$	T $055°$	T $150°$
V $012°$ W	V $005°$ W	V $029°$ E	V $014°$ W	V $023°$ W
M $147°$	M $025°$	M $046°$	M $069°$	M $173°$
D $006°$ W	D $002°$ E	D $002°$ W	D $007°$ E	D $002°$ E
C $153°$	C $023°$	C $048°$	C $062°$	C $171°$

11	12	13	14	15
T $104°$	T $080°$	T $021°$	T $060°$	T $323°$
V $010°$ W	V $022°$ E	V $012°$ W	V $011°$ W	V $012°$ W
M $114°$	M $058°$	M $033°$	M $071°$	M $335°$
D $002°$ E	D $003°$ W	D $009°$ W	D $006°$ E	D $006°$ E
C $112°$	C $061°$	C $042°$	C $065°$	C $329°$

16	17	18	19	20
T $175°$	See	C $270°$	C $237°$	C $155°$
V $021°$ W	Figure	D $004°$ W	D $001°$ E	D $004°$ E
M $196°$	14	M $266°$	M $238°$	M $159°$
D $002°$ W		V $012°$ E	V $014°$ W	V $008°$ W
C $198°$		T $278°$	T $224°$	T $151°$

Captain Jack's Basic Navigation, *By Jack I. Davis*

21
C 168°
D 006° W
M 162°
V 008° W
T 154°

22
C 076°
D 000°
M 076°
V 005° W
T 071°

23
C 153°
D 003° W
M 150°
V 012° E
T 162°

24
C 228°
D 003° E
M 231°
V 023° E
T 254°

25
C 120°
D 002°.5 E
M 122°.5 E
V 022°.5' E
T 145°

26
C 071°
D 006° E
M 077°
V 002° W
T 075°

27
C 034°
D 010° W
M 024°
V 020° W
T 004°

28
C 081°
D 010° W
M 071°
V 019° E
T 090°

29
C 175°
D 002° E
M 177°
V 000°
T 177°

30
C 054°
D 005° E
M 059°
V 010° W
T 049°

31
C 235°
D 007° W
M 228°
V 004° E
T 232°

32
C 058°
D 004° E
M 062°
V 000°
T 062°

33
C 178°
D 022° E
M 200°
V 000°
T 200°

34
C 091°
D 001° E
M 092°
V 008° W
T 084°

35
C 015°
D 026° W
M 349°
V 021° E
T 010°

36
See Figure 15

37
T 000°
V 012° W
M 012°
D 007° E
C 005°

38
T 360°
V 016° E
M 344°
D 016° E
C 328°

Figure 14

Answer for 17. The key phrase is "over the stern!"

111° true
180° reciprocal
291° true boat course - Then   T   291°
                                                     V   006°.5' W
                                                     M   297°.5
                                                     D   000°
                                                     C   297°.5

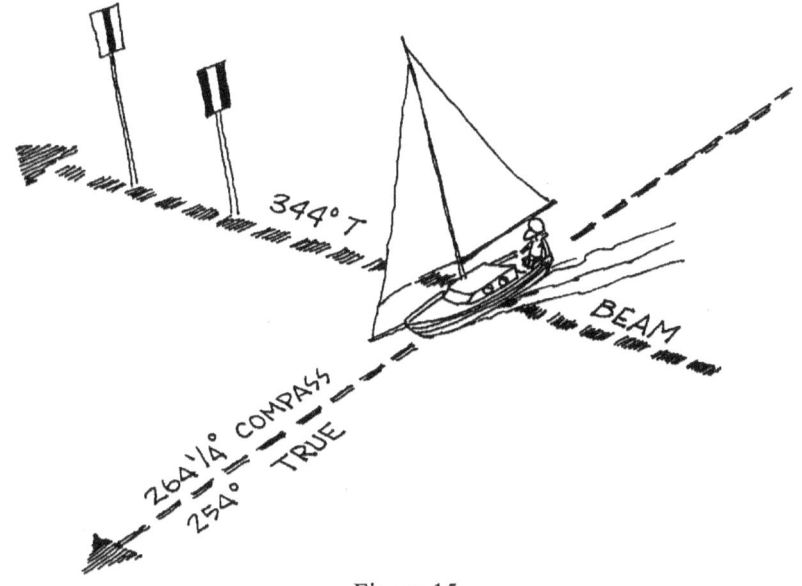

Figure 15

Answer to 36. Beam is a hypothetical line at a 90° angle to keel. If you were going north, the beam would run east and west.

       344°   C   264°.25
   -90° Beam   D   003° W
       254°   M   261°.25
                            V   007°.25 W
                            T   254°

Captain Jack's Basic Navigation, By Jack I. Davis

Chapter 4
TO BE A BETTER SAILOR

There are sailors and then there are sailors. As with any endeavor, the more time and effort you put into it, the better and more proficient you become.

In most sports, like golf or bowling, the person who spends the most time practicing is usually the better athlete.

With sailing, practice helps, to a point. When something happens that you have not practiced, or even contemplated, you may be in trouble. You must know what you are going to do in any situation that could arise, even though you have never practiced the procedure.

There is no way to prepare for every eventuality, but you can read the stories of the hundreds of sailors who have gone before you. You can read about their storms, their groundings, what someone did when the mast fell, the sails blew out or their water supply became contaminated.

In one of Erick Hiscock's stories, he explains sailing off the anchor, which at that time had not occurred to me. He was in a remote anchorage in the South Pacific and when he was ready to leave, the engine would not start. He described his tactic of raising the main and tacking back and forth until he sailed across the anchor, at which time he could break it loose and continue on.

With his book open to that passage, I took my boat out

and dropped anchor. Following his instructions, I sailed off the anchor. That maneuver then became a standard part of my sailing instructions and I always try to relate the story of how I learned it.

I have read about the "Hove To" maneuver, not only in the Hiscock books, but in many other stories by circumnavigators. I was well convinced of the viability of the tactic before I ever tried it.

There are tactics and procedures in stories that I do not agree with, usually because another writer or circumstance has convinced me otherwise. A good example is the sea anchor. There are sailors who swear by the sea anchor and others who swear at them. Certainly the folks who manufacture and sell sea anchors laud them to high heaven, but there are other opinions I respect more.

When I thought of the sea anchor controversy, I had to look carefully at both sides of the debate. Then with my own experiences added to the mix, I was convinced that I would never allow a sea anchor aboard my vessel.

I could rehash this debate but I would only be covering well trotted ground. I suggest reading all you can find on the issue to form your own opinion.

This kind of debate is the exception and not the rule in sailing. Sailing goes far back into history and although there have been some changes through the years, in reality, not much has changed. Most tactics were old hat to sailors hundreds of years ago and therefore there is a proper way to do most everything on a sailboat.

In addition to the Hiscocks, another couple have written several books about their sailing adventures, Len and Larry Pardee. They advocate going small, going inexpensive and going now! Although I don't agree with their Spartan sailing lifestyle, there is much to be said for smaller boats.

There are other books that are not as much fun to read but which you should study; *Chapman's Navigation & Small Boat Handling* is one. I have had a copy aboard for many years and still refer to it often. *Annapolis Book of Seamanship* is another.

You should have a copy of the *United States Coast Pilot #5*. This is a government publication covering a multitude of information not shown on charts or elsewhere.

If you really get serious about your nautical education, you should have *Dutton's Navigation & Piloting* and *Bowditch's American Practical Navigator, Volumes I and II.* I would only recommend *Bowditch's American Practical Navigator, Volume II* for the tables it includes until you have a considerable amount of experience. Until that time, these books have a tendency to tell you more than you need to know.

In my case, I have too many books. Two or three more and my boat may sink and this is a problem for most long-term cruisers. You want to have books aboard to cover everything, but this cannot be.

Captain Jack's Basic Navigation, By Jack I. Davis

Chapter 5
DISTANCE OF THE HORIZON

Most of the dangerous navigational problems come about when land is either in sight or some object on land is in sight. I am asked repeatedly, "Are you frightened at being in the middle of the ocean?" The answer, of course, is no. I start to become uneasy (if not frightened) when I get close to land.

When you are sailing in the middle of an ocean or far away from land, there is very little that can do you harm. Close to land there are many things that can do you in; rocks or coral heads, for instance.

One of the important navigational talents is to see a tall object on land and determine how far away it is. The earth is a big round ball with the surface curvature symmetrical. When you are sitting on a boat with your eye level at seven feet above the water, the horizon is always 3.1 nautical miles away.

The following is the mathematical formula that gives us the information in Table 2. This formula is calculating for distance in nautical miles.

Distance = 1.17 x the square root of the height of eye.
As an example: If the height of the eye is 10 feet.
The square root of 10 is 3.1622776. Multiply this figure by 1.17 and the result is the distance to the *horizon* or 3.6998648 which you would round off to 3.7 nautical miles.

The second part of the formula is the same only this time the height of the object is substituted for the height of eye.

Distance = 1.17 x the square root of the height of the object.

As an example: If the height of the object is 30 feet.

The square root of 30 is 5.4772255. Multiply this figure by 1.17 and the result is 6.4083539 which you would round off to 6.4.

3.7 = 1.17 x the square root of the 10.

6.4 = 1.17 x the square root of the 30. Add the two distance answers (3.7 nm) + (6.4 nm) and the sum (10.1 nm) will equal the distance off the object when it is first sighted.

You can use Table 2 as a quick reference. The distances in the table have been calculated for distance away for both height of eye and height of objects.

The table and the formula will provide accurate answers only when the sea is completely flat. Riding the crest of a wave will effect the distances as will being in the trough of a wave. Furthermore, for your safety, never assume the table or the formula will provide more than an approximation of the actual distance.

All nautical charts showing the approaches to land show the height of most significant objects along the shore. The Coast Guard has another publication called the *Light List* which shows the height of all aids to navigation, such as range markers, light towers and the luminous range of a light atop the object.

Luminous Range - The distance the object may be seen on a clear night without regard to curvature of the earth. The light may be bright enough to be seen 25 miles away but at that distance it would be below the horizon. Inversely, the object is high enough to be seen 25 miles away but the light only has a luminous range of 10 miles.

Captain Jack's Basic Navigation, By Jack I. Davis

DISTANCE OF THE HORIZON

Height Feet	Nautical Miles	Statute Miles	Height Feet	Nautical Miles	Statute Miles
1	1.2	1.3	38	7.2	8.3
2	1.7	1.9	39	7.3	8.4
3	2	2.3	40	7.4	8.5
4	2.3	2.7	41	7.5	8.6
5	2.6	3	42	7.6	8.7
6	2.9	3.3	43	7.7	8.8
7	3.1	3.6	44	7.8	8.9
8	3.3	3.8	45	7.8	9
9	3.5	4	46	7.9	9.1
10	3.7	4.3	47	8	9.2
11	3.9	4.5	48	8.1	9.3
12	4.1	4.7	49	8.2	9.4
13	4.2	4.9	50	8.3	9.5
14	4.4	5	55	8.7	10
15	4.5	5.2	60	9.1	10.4
16	4.7	5.4	65	9.4	10.9
17	4.8	5.6	70	9.8	11.3
18	5	5.7	75	10.1	11.7
19	5.1	5.9	80	10.5	12
20	5.2	6	85	10.8	12.4
21	5.4	6.2	90	11.1	12.8
22	5.5	6.3	95	11.4	13.1
2	5.6	6.5	100	11.7	13.5
24	5.7	6.6	105	12	13.8
25	5.9	6.7	110	12.3	14.1
26	6	6.9	115	12.5	14.4
27	6.1	7	120	12.8	14.7
28	6.2	7.1	125	13.1	15.1
29	6.3	7.4	130	13.3	15.4
30	6.4	7.5	135	13.6	15.6
31	6.5	7.6	140	13.8	15.9
32	6.6	7.7	145	14.1	16.2
33	6.7	7.9	150	14.3	16.5
34	6.8	8	160	14.8	17
35	6.9	8.1	170	15.3	17.6
36	7	8.2	180	15.7	18.1

Table 2 BFP

Only <u>distances</u> can be added or subtracted in Table 2. Never add or subtract heights. If your height of eye is ten feet

Captain Jack's Basic Navigation, By Jack I. Davis

(3.7 nm) and the height of an object is 20 feet (5.2 nm), you add the distances together and they equal 8.9 miles, which is correct. If you were to add the two heights together to total 30 feet, the answer would be 6.4 miles, which is wrong.

Many times at sea with students aboard, I have demonstrated "Bobbing The Light". This occurs when we are nearing a landfall and we know an object of a certain height with a light on top is near our landfall. When we first spot the light, we can be reasonably sure of our distance away using the formula or table. To double check your answer, you sit down and the light will go out of sight. When you stand up the light is in sight, thus "Bobbing The Light". See figures 16 and 16a.

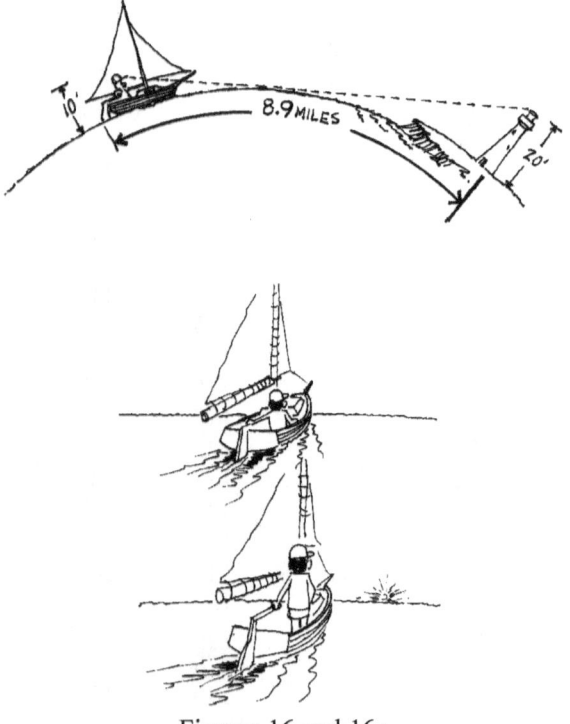

Figures 16 and 16a

Standing, the light is visible. Sitting it is not.

Captain Jack's Basic Navigation, By Jack I. Davis

The following problems will give you an opportunity to be certain you understand the proper methods for using the table and the formula. You will notice some questions use a height that is not in the table. You must use the formula or a combination of the formula and the table to achieve the correct answer for these questions. The answers are at the end of the chapter.

1. You sight a 780 foot mountain peak just clearing the horizon. If your height of eye is 15 feet, what is your distance away _____?

2. Assuming good visibility, how far is each light visible for the height of eye shown.

    a. 300 foot oil rig. Height of eye: 20 feet. _____?

    b. 200 foot smoke stack. Height of eye: 60 feet. _____?

    c. 220 foot radio tower. Height of eye: 12 feet. _____?

    d. 110 foot TV tower. Height of eye: 12 feet. _____?

    e. 200 foot tank. Height of eye: 10 feet. _____?

3. A navigational light 120 feet above sea level has a charted range of 20 miles. What must your height of eye be to see this light at its charted range _____?

4. A light 115 feet high to an observer at sea level compared to a light 100 feet high to an observer with a height of eye of 15 feet _____?

5. On a clear dark night, you identify a light just breaking

clear of the horizon. The light is 75 feet high with a charted range of 20 nm. Your height of eye is 50 feet. What is your distance from the light _____?

6. A lookout with a height of eye of 55 feet observes a flashing light on the horizon. The light is timed and identified as a navigational light 117 feet above sea level. How far was the vessel from the light when first observed _____?

7. To what distance does the sea horizon extend if your height of eye is 8 feet _____?

8. What is the horizon distance for each of the heights:

   a. 34 feet _____?

   b. 115 feet _____?

   c. 180 feet _____?

9. At what distance should you be able to see each of these strong lights:

HEIGHT OF LIGHT	HEIGHT OF EYE	
a. 150 feet	30 feet	?
b. 110 feet	80 feet	?
c. 300 feet	30 feet	?
d. 540 feet	40 feet	?
e. 720 feet	45 feet	?

10. At what distance can you see a light whose height is 150 feet, and charted range is 19 nm? Your height of eye is 42 feet. _____?

DISTANCE OF THE HORIZON ANSWERS

1. 32.7 + 4.5 = 37.2 nm

2.
   a. 20.3 + 5.2 = 25.5 nm

   b. 16.5 + 9.1 = 25.6 nm

   c. 17.4 + 4.1 = 21.5 nm

   d. 12.3 + 4.1 = 16.4 nm

   e. 16.5 + 3.7 = 20.2 nm

3. 12.8 + x = 20, x = 7.2 i.e. height of eye of 38 feet.

4. 11.7 + 4.5 = 16.2
           - 12.5
             3.7

5. 10.1 + 8.3 = 18.4 nm (which is less than charted range)

6. 115'   12.5
      55'   8.7
       2'   1.7
            22.9 nm

Captain Jack's Basic Navigation, By Jack I. Davis

This is one of the situations where using the table correctly provides the wrong answer. Mathematical tables are not infallible. Adding the additional 2 feet of height to the light to equal 117 (the table shows 115 and 120) produces a quirk. Obviously you can not be farther off using a light of 117 feet than you would be using a light of 120 feet but using the table correctly shows you are by 1.56 nm. When in doubt, use the next lower number (in this case, 115 feet) in the table in place of adding numbers to achieve a number which is not listed. You could also use the formula, discussed earlier, to achieve the correct answer of 21.34 nautical miles off.

7. 8.0 = 3.3 nm

8.
   a. 34 feet = 6.8

   b. 115 feet = 12.5

   c. 180 feet = 15.7

9.
   a. 20.7

   b. 22.8

   c. 26.7

   d. 34.6

   e. 39.2

10. 150' = 14.3
    42' = 7.6
       21.9 but the Luminous range is 19 nm.

Chapter 6
HEAVY WEATHER SAILING

A well found sailing vessel with an experienced crew can handle almost anything that comes down upon it. I don't want to dwell on the frightening aspects of an otherwise extremely pleasant experience, but there are some things you should know.

There are numerous books available on storm tending and I recommend you read several to expose yourself to different opinions. But let me give you my storm tending philosophy by first relating a story.

Several years ago, an English cruising couple by the name of Erick and Susan Hiscock were sailing down the east coast of the United States after having sailed around the world several times. By this time they had become the most famous cruising couple in the world.

They had written many excellent books about their adventures and numerous articles about sailing for sailing magazines. A yacht club in the Miami area heard they were nearby, hunted them down, and invited them to come in and give a talk for the club's membership.

This they did and upon arriving at the club, Erick asked the master of ceremonies what topic he and Susan should discuss. "How about Heavy Weather Sailing," the emcee said. "But Sir," Erick replied, "Susan and I do not sail in heavy weather."

Which brings me to my point. The Hiscocks watched the seasonal weather very closely and were not about to be caught in a major weather system, except in the rarest of circumstances. In those very rare cases where they were intercepted by violent weather they simply hove-to. In this maneuver, if under sail, you bring your vessel through the wind as if you were going to tack, but without bringing the jib across. After the bow passes through the wind and the jib is back-winded, you then turn the helm all the way over toward the back-winded jib.

Figure 29

Hove-To

When Hove-To, the wind is from the starboard side. The helm is turned to make a starboard turn. The jib sheet remains on the starboard side.

The boat, at that point, is trying to sail into the back-winded jib. It reaches a point of equilibrium and, in effect, is stopped except for a slight amount of leeway.

You can do this with main and jib in winds of forty knots. In heavier winds, you drop the sails, turn the helm hard over and lock it down. You are effectively hove-to, under bare poles.

Several of the most distinguished and capable sailors in the world have used this technique and have written about it. I personally have used it hundreds of times.

On one delivery, I was bringing a new thirty-nine foot Beneteau from Pensacola to Galveston. The vessel had one 130 jib and a standard main without reef points. Normally, I would not have gone to sea without better sail resources but it was a short trip and my better judgment failed me.

About fourteen hours after rounding the Mississippi Delta, on a northwesterly course, we were hit by a winter weather front with winds building to about fifty knots. We dropped the jib and tried to continue with the main alone, but we were overpowered.

We dropped and secured the main, turned the helm hard over and locked it down. We also secured the wheel with a line to be certain the wheel brake didn't slip. We laid ahull for twenty-seven hours with the winds of fifty knots gusting to sixty knots.

After the winds began to let up, we checked our position and found we had been pushed south twenty-four miles in the twenty-seven hours we were hove-to. This meant our leeway was less than one knot. Although it wasn't a pleasant experience, there was no damage to the boat and the crew could rest in between drinking coffee and playing gin.

I could tell hove-to stories for the next hundred pages but let me end with one more story.

I was called into a charter company as a visiting instructor. The concept was a corporation team building exercise of learning to sail. There were groups of four students and one instructor on each of ten different boats. Each group was more or less competing with the other groups.

Captain Jack's Basic Navigation, By Jack I. Davis

Prior to the beginning of this exercise, the ten captains had a meeting with the charter operator to discuss plans. They covered starting time, return time and the schedule; two hours of tacking and jibing, anchor drill, etc. I brought up the suggestion of showing the students the hove-to maneuver which I consider to be the most important lesson in sailing. To my great surprise, the other nine instructors didn't teach the maneuver and I don't think many of them understood the concept.

When you take sailing lessons, be certain this maneuver is included, or go out and try it for yourself.

In previous chapters I mentioned my dislike of sea anchors and I will say it again: I don't like or use sea anchors or warps.

In theory, a sea-anchor attached to the bow in storm conditions will hold the bow into the wind, giving the vessel a better ride. The error in this thinking is that a sailboat attached to a sea anchor (or anchor for that matter) will stay straight into the wind. It just doesn't happen.

The main problem is the tremendous forces the sea anchor puts on the boat, so much so that cleats can be torn out and other gear damaged.

The bottom line is that a vessel hove-to will ride better, safer and with less potential damage than a vessel attached to a sea anchor. Provided land is not nearby to leeward, I feel this is the safest method to use when riding out a storm.

I saw a sailboat that had been tied to an offshore drilling platform's mooring buoy during a fifty knot blow. The owner's thinking was that the mooring buoy would hold his bow into the wind (like a sea-anchor), and would be a safe place to ride out the storm. The vessel was virtually destroyed and was ultimately considered a complete loss by the insurance company.

Warps are lines strung behind your boat to help reduce your speed when your running off before a storm. My first question is why run off before a storm? If the storm is that violent, why not hove-to? If there is some logical reason to run down wind in heavy weather, then running without the warps is much safer. There have been several cases of boats pitchpoling when running off trailing warps.

The real keys to handling weather at sea are to have a good inventory of sails and storm sails, know when to use them and have a plan for whatever conditions you might encounter.

Captain Jack's Basic Navigation, By Jack I. Davis

Chapter 7
BOW AND BEAM BEARINGS

Distances at sea and along the coast are eminently hard to judge. Like the *Distance of the Horizon* procedure we discussed earlier, it is very helpful to have a tool to determine our distance from an object we are either passing at sea or along the shore.

If we are passing an object, like a drilling platform that is not directly on our course, we can obtain a close approximation of the distance to that object, when we are abeam.

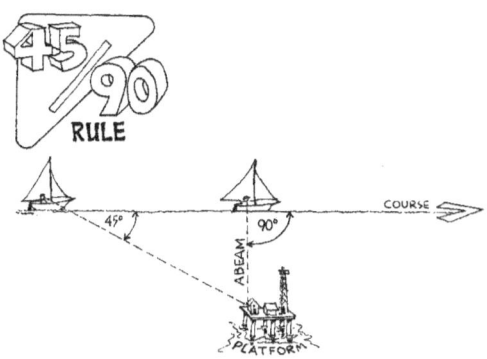

Figure 17

45/90 Rule
Distance Run Equals Distance Abeam

The distance run between 1st and 2nd bearings will be the distance off when abeam. This means, while you are passing an object at sea and it is noted to be forty-five degrees off the bow at one point, and ninety degrees off the bow at another point, then the distance you traveled between the first point and the second point is the distance you are away from the object when you reach the second point.

Figure 17 gives you an example of the 45/90 rule. Thinking back to your high school geometry days, what is described is an isosceles right triangle.

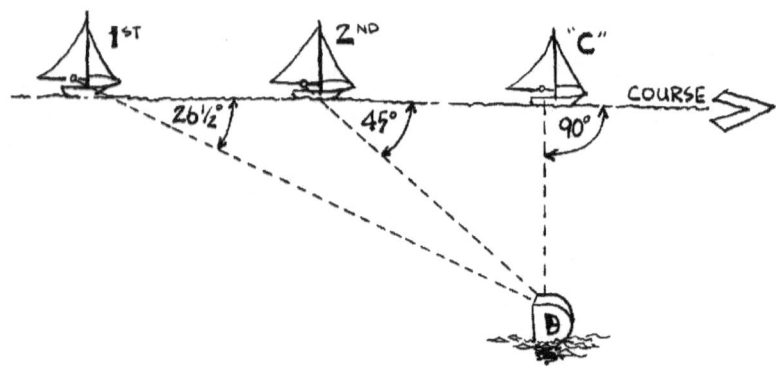

Figure 18

26.5 / 45 Rule

The 26.5°/45° rule differs from the 45°/90° rule in that it is making a prediction about an event that will occur in the future. It is telling us how far away an object will be long before the object is abeam. This conceivably, could alert you to a change of course, if when abeam, you will be closer to the object than you will want to be.

Double The Angle On The Bow

The Distance Run Is The Distance Off At The Time Of The Second Bearing

This rule basically falls into the same category as the 45/90 rule even though I show it separately. When you take any bearing angle (Not compass heading) and then later take a second bearing that is double the first, the distance run from the first bearing to the second bearing is the distance off at the second bearing.

As an example. You are on a compass heading of $010°$. You see a light at a bearing of $055°$ ($45°$ off the bow) You continue on the $010°$ compass course until the compass bearing of the light is $100°$ ($90°$ off the bow) You have doubled the angle on the bow between the $055°$ reading and the $100°$ reading. The distance you run during that time is the distance away from the light at the time of the second reading.

One more bearing that you must learn is the bearing to another boat approaching your vessel from port or starboard. Using this procedure correctly will tell you if the oncoming boat will pass in front of your boat, behind your boat or pass right through the saloon of your boat. The steps are as follows.

While maintaining a constant compass course, take a relative bearing of the other boat.

If the relative bearing moves toward the bow, the boat will pass ahead of you.

If the relative bearing moves toward the stern, the boat will pass behind you.

If the relative bearing remains the same, you are about to have guests for dinner!

The above will only give a true answer if the other boat has maintained a constant compass course as well. Any deviation in the path of either boat will render the process useless.

Now for some problems to test your understanding of Bow and Beam Bearings.

Captain Jack's Basic Navigation, By Jack I. Davis

1. You take a bearing of a light house that is 45° off the bow and again when it is abeam. The distance run between the two bearings is 4 nm. How far are you off the lighthouse when abeam _____?

2. At 1020 hours a vessel making 15 kn sighted a light bearing 45° on the port bow. The light was abeam at 1105 hours and was how far off _____?

3. A vessel proceeding on a course of 000° at a speed of 12 kn observes a light bearing 045° from the bow at 1015 hours. At 1130 hours the light is abeam and is how far off _____?

4. A light bears 45° off the bow at 1000 hours and is abeam at 1045 hours. Your boat's speed is 12 kn. What is your distance off the light at 1045 hours _____?

5. Running at 12 knots, a light bears 45° off the bow at 1955 hours and is abeam at 2105. How far off the light are you when abeam _____?

6. A vessel on a course of 090° at 12 kn, takes a bearing on a lighthouse at 135°, and 10 minutes later at 180°. How far away is the lighthouse at the time of the second bearing _____?

7. You steer 000° T at 14 kn in a current setting 180° T at a drift of 2 kn. You run 20 minutes between a bow and beam bearing on a light. How far are you off the light when abeam _____?

8. A vessel sights a light bearing 045° off the bow. Holding her course, she travels 5 nm until the light bears 090° off the port bow. How far is the vessel off the light at the time of the second bearing _____?

68

9. A vessel on course 195° passes light "A" abeam to starboard at 1427 hours. At 1542 hours buoy "B" bears 150° and at 1551 hours is passed abeam to port. The distance from abeam light "A" to abeam buoy "B" is 22.4 nm. The distance off buoy "B" when abeam was _____ ?

Draw a diagram, plotting all the facts of the problem. This will help solve the problem.

10. At 1010 hours a lighthouse bore 26.5° off the bow and 1022 hours it bore 045° off the bow. The vessel is making 10 kn, with no current. The vessel's distance from the lighthouse when abeam will be _____ ? (26.5°/45° Rule)

11. The speed of a boat is 8 kn. A lighthouse is 26.5° off the bow at 1000 hours and 45° at 1030 hours. When it is abeam, the lighthouse will be how far off _____ ?

12. The first bearing is a shore light that was 26.5° on the starboard bow at 1900 hours. At 1940 hours, a second bearing of 45° on the starboard bow was taken. Speed is 15 kn. The light will be abeam at _____ ? and will be how many miles off _____ ?

13. A vessel sights a light bearing 26.5° off the port bow. Holding her course she travels 5 nm. The light bears 45° off the port bow. How far will the vessel be off the light when the light is abeam, if she holds her course and speed _____ ?

14. A vessel sights a light 25° off the starboard bow. She holds course and travels 5 nm when the light bears 50° of her starboard bow. How far is the vessel off the light at the time of the second bearing _____ ? Double the angle on the bow.

15. A vessel is on course 185° true, speed 10 kn. A light is observed bearing 155° true at 1020 hours. At 1105 hours the

light bears 125° true. The distance off at 1105 hours is _____?

16. You are underway at 12 kn with no current or leeway. You see a lighthouse and take a bearing at 1130 hours of 28° off the port bow. At 1201 hours, you take a second bearing which reads 68° off your port bow. How far off at the second bearing _____? How far off will you be at closest approach _____?

Bowditch Volume II, *Table 7* uses any two bearings to determine the distance off at the second bearing and the prediction of the distance off when abeam. This book is a worthwhile purchase to avoid using the formulas that follow.

You can use the following formulae to calculate the distance off at any angle by solving plane and oblique triangles. This is the only set of formulas in this book which require a scientific calculator and higher math skills.

In a right plane triangle you must substitute only the values representing the basic triangle in the appropriate formulas and solve. It then follows, if a and b are known:

$\tan A = a/b$ Oblique plane triangles:
$B = 90 - A$ Law of sines:
$c = a \cos A$ $\dfrac{a}{\sin A} = \dfrac{b}{\sin B} = \dfrac{c}{\sin C}$

If c and B are given:
$A = 90 - B$ Law of cosines
$a = c \sin A$ $a^2 = b^2 + c^2 - 2bc \cos A$
$b = c \cos A$

Captain Jack's Basic Navigation, By Jack I. Davis

BOW AND BEAM ANSWERS

Captain Jack's Basic Navigation, By Jack I. Davis

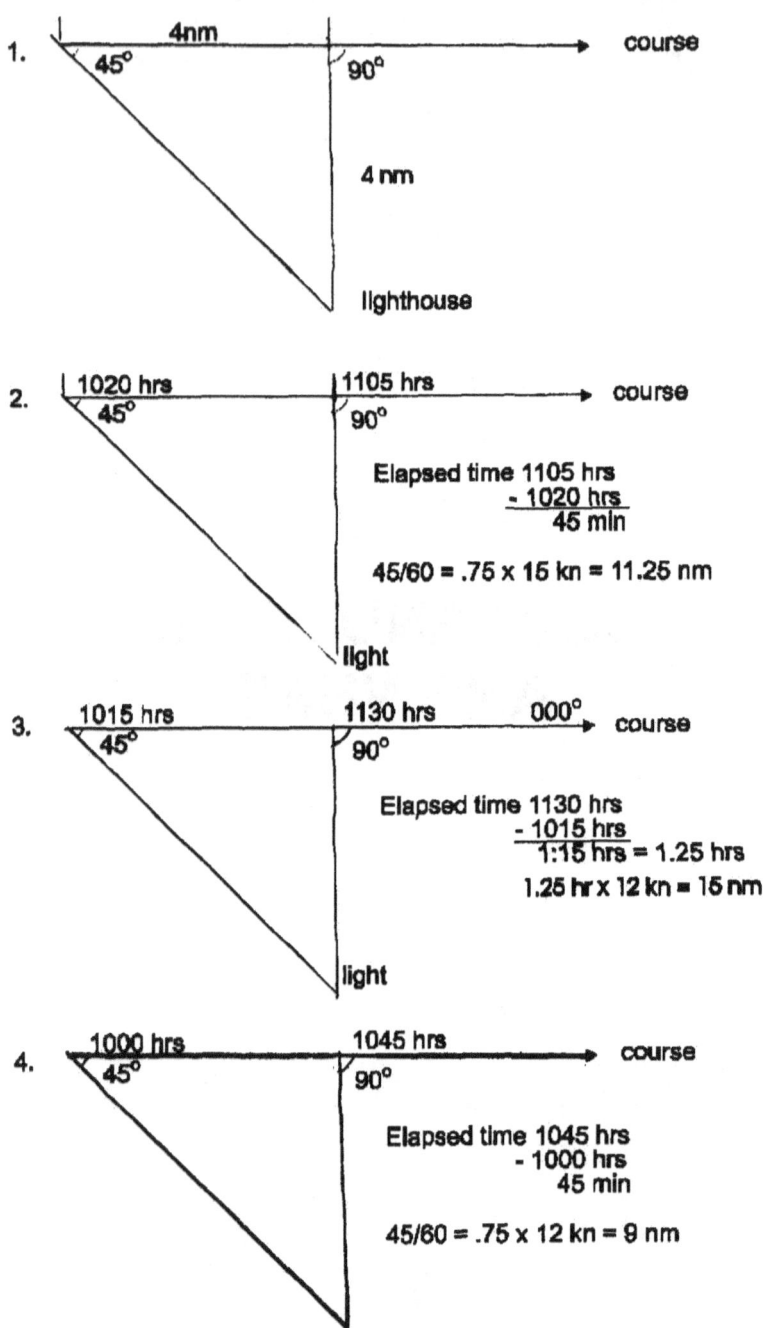

Captain Jack's Basic Navigation, By Jack I. Davis

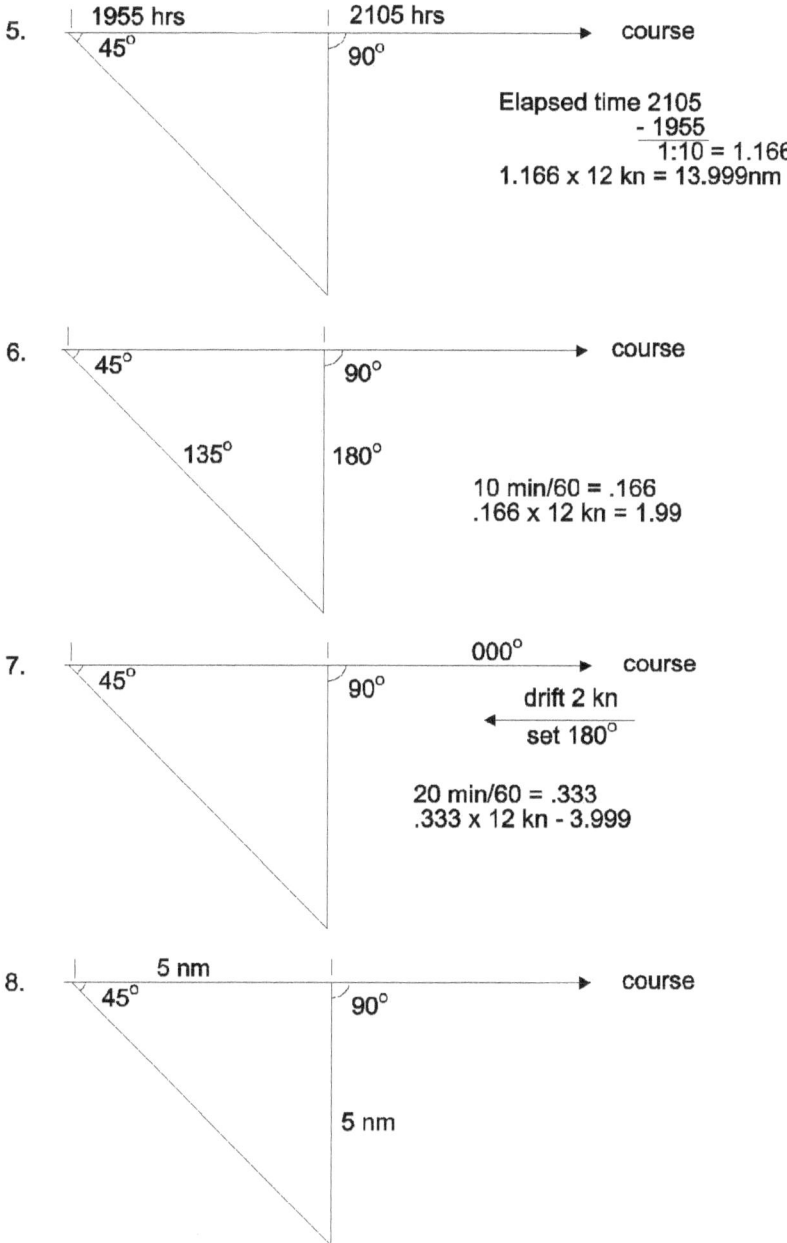

5. 1955 hrs | 2105 hrs → course
   45° | 90°

   Elapsed time 2105
   − 1955
   1:10 = 1.166
   1.166 x 12 kn = 13.999nm

6. 45° | 90° → course
   135° | 180°

   10 min/60 = .166
   .166 x 12 kn = 1.99

7. 45° | 90°   000° → course
   drift 2 kn
   ← set 180°

   20 min/60 = .333
   .333 x 12 kn − 3.999

8. 5 nm
   45° | 90° → course
   5 nm

Captain Jack's Basic Navigation, By Jack I. Davis

9.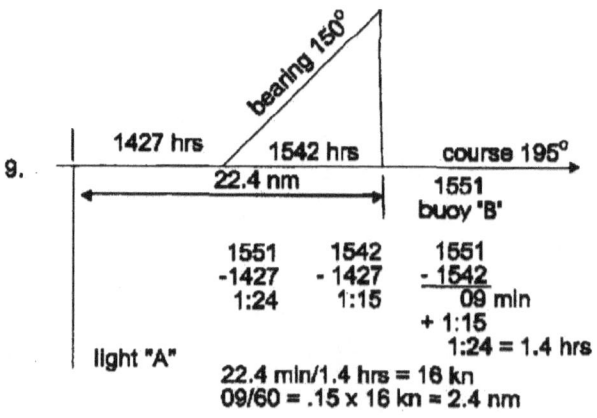

10.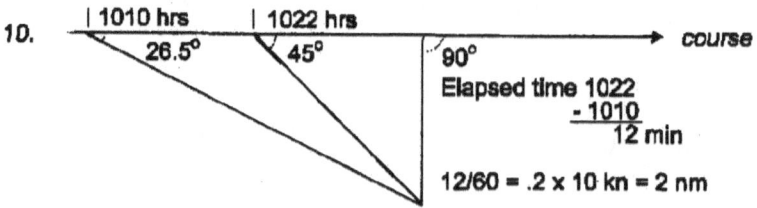

11.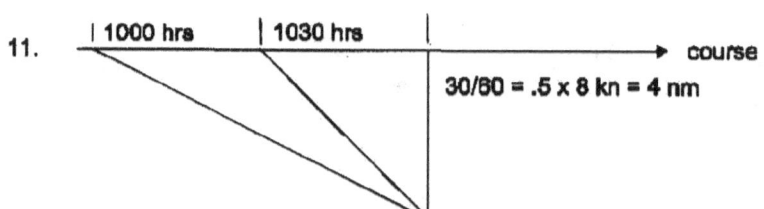

Captain Jack's Basic Navigation, By Jack I. Davis

12.

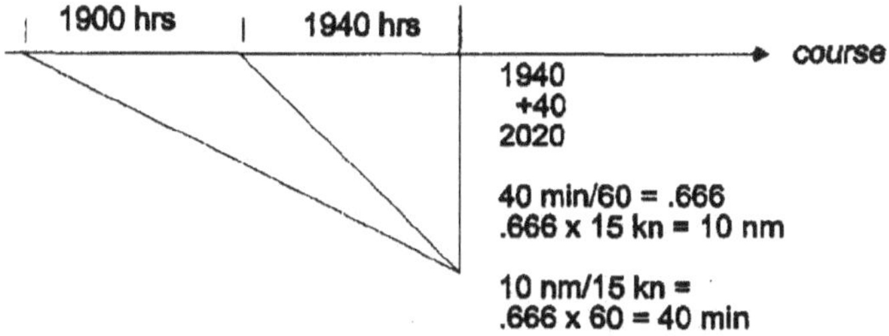

```
1900 hrs    1940 hrs
                                                    course
            1940
            +40
            2020

            40 min/60 = .666
            .666 x 15 kn = 10 nm

            10 nm/15 kn =
            .666 x 60 = 40 min
```

13.

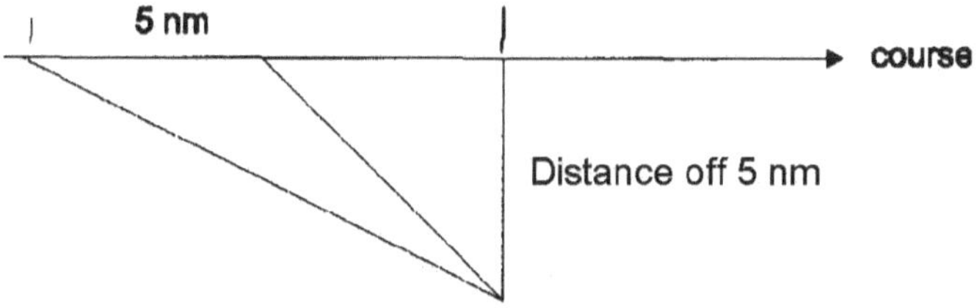

```
    5 nm
                                                    course

            Distance off 5 nm
```

14.

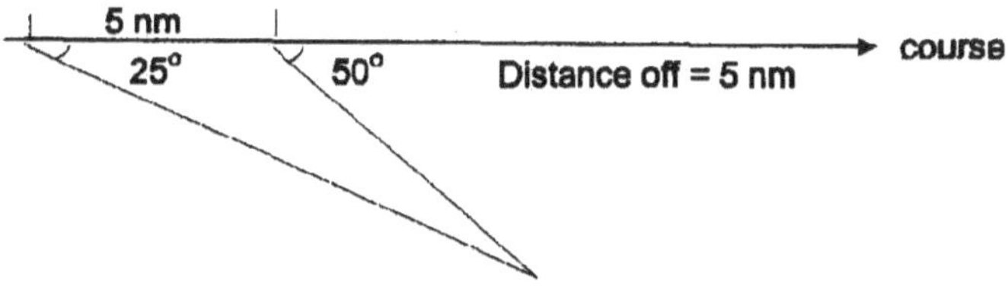

```
   5 nm
   25°    50°    Distance off = 5 nm         course
```

15.

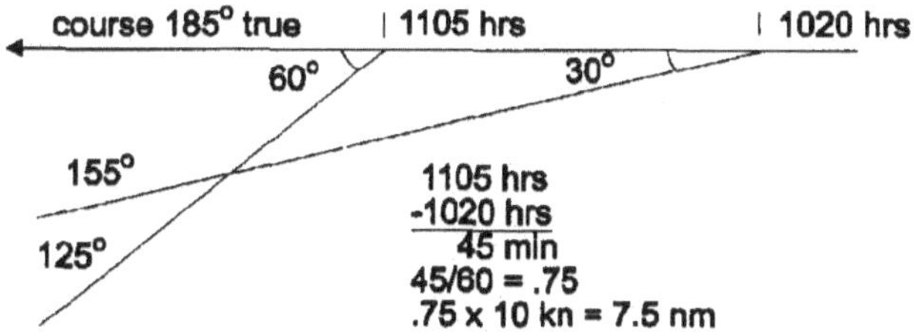

course 185° true   1105 hrs   1020 hrs
         60°   30°
155°
         1105 hrs
125°   -1020 hrs
         45 min
         45/60 = .75
         .75 x 10 kn = 7.5 nm

75

Captain Jack's Basic Navigation, By Jack I. Davis

16.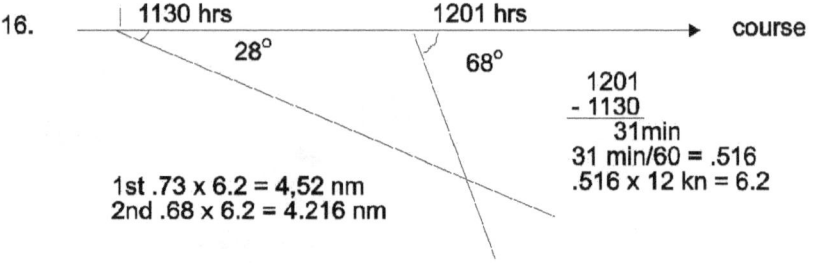

1st .73 x 6.2 = 4,52 nm
2nd .68 x 6.2 = 4.216 nm

```
 1201
-1130
 31min
31 min/60 = .516
.516 x 12 kn = 6.2
```

Chapter 8
LEARN TO MANEUVER YOUR BOAT

Since most boat damage occurs while docking, leaving the dock or other maneuvers in close quarters, it is imperative to learn how to make your boat do what you want it to do while motoring.

Handling a sailboat, of almost any size, with a single inboard engine is very deceptive when you consider windage, current and the vessel's turning radius. Unfortunately, most newcomers to sailing do not place a high priority on something as mundane as driving around in a sailboat under power.

There are also many long-term sailors who have never learned the ABCs of sailboat maneuvering. Therefore, they get into all kinds of trouble, particularly when wind and current become a factor.

The primary concept in close quarters maneuvering is the effect of torque on your vessel. Your propeller is a screw working its way through the water. Torque is a pulling force, to the side, while your propeller is spinning (prop walk).

In forward gear the force of the prop wash over the rudder gives you control and turning ability and the effect of torque is relatively unimportant. In reverse, there is no rush of water over the rudder and torque will have a tremendous effect.

You can demonstrate this with your boat tied at the dock. Put your engine in reverse at a moderate idle. You will see that, in addition to the backward movement of the boat, there is also a movement to the side, the stern will move to starboard or port. Seventy-five percent of the boats I've been on, the torque in reverse, pulled the stern to port.

When you cast off and start to back out of a slip, the stern of the boat will be pulled to this torque side regardless of what you do with the rudder. Since the prop's wash is forward, there is no water movement over the rudder. The boat speed must reach a point where there is enough water going over the rudder to offset the torque effect, thereby giving some rudder control.

If the torque is to port in reverse, the stern of the boat is going to port. Trying to move the stern to starboard is almost hopeless. You can build speed to gain rudder control, but in many marinas the extra room just doesn't exist.

If you don't have the extra room, let the stern go to port and then make a 270 degree turn, which is easy if you let the torque help.

Back up so your bow clears any pilings, then go to forward gear and accelerate to a moderate idle. Do not turn the helm until you have prop wash over the rudder. (If the boat is moving backward at speed and you turn the helm, the boat will respond to the helm).

When you have forward movement, turn the helm hard over in the direction you want to go. Don't allow excess speed to build. When you reach a fair amount of forward movement, pull the gear shift back into reverse (All sailboat marine gears that I have used are safe to shift at a moderate idle without slowing the engine or stopping in neutral). Remember, the helm is hard over, just leave it alone.

With your boat in reverse, the torque is pulling your stern to the side and helping with your turn. Remain in reverse until the boat is completely stopped. The boat will continue to turn. When you feel the turn slowing and before the boat movement is astern, shift to forward.

If you continue this procedure, the boat will turn, almost on its own axis. It is not unusual for me to have a student turning a thirty-three foot boat in a 45 foot fairway after less than one hour's practice.

If the wind or current is strong, you may need to increase the RPM on your engine to offset the leeway.

Once you understand torque, make it your friend not your enemy.

Captain Jack's Basic Navigation, By Jack I. Davis

Chapter 9
CHART READING

    Learning to read a nautical chart is very much like the experience you went through when you saw your first automobile road map. It can be very intimidating to look at all the little squiggles you do not understand. After you learn the basics, the road map is not so intimidating. In fact, it becomes your friend and opens a whole new world for you, allowing you to plan a trip and go almost anywhere.

    The nautical chart also is intimidating at first. After you understand the basics it is as easy to use as a road map, and it too opens a new world for you. More so than the road map, because you have fewer limitations.

    A nautical chart is a graphic representation on a flat surface, of a navigable portion of the earth's surface. A chart shows the depth of water by numerous soundings, and sometimes by soundings and depth contours, which is a line that joins points of equal depth. This is often shown as a dotted line.

    In the lower left or right corners of the chart will be a legend stating how the chart's depths are measured. This may be in fathoms, feet or meters. If you look at a coastal chart giving the depth in fathoms, you may see these dotted lines at the ten, fifty and one hundred fathom areas.

    Fathom - A fathom was once considered to be the height

of a typical sailor, which at one time was probably about five feet. In more recent times the fathom, by convention, was standardized at six feet.

Marine charts also show the shoreline of adjacent land, topographic features that serve as landmarks, aids to navigation, dangers to navigation and other information of interest to mariners.

You will also find on the chart the fractional scale or chart scale. This can be shown as a representative fraction or as a numerical scale.

In the representative fraction, the scale may be 1:2500. This would be one inch on the chart to 2500 inches in the real world. In other words, if this is a chart of a small bay, one inch on the chart would equal about two hundred and eight feet on the bay.

The 1:2500 chart is known as a large scale chart, as the one inch is large in relation to the 2500 inches. This scale covers a very small area.

A scale of 1:14,000,000 (one inch to 194 miles), is known as a small scale chart and these charts cover a very large area. They are generally used for voyage planning and offshore purposes so you would switch to a larger scale chart (covering a small area) when approaching pilot waters.

Confusing isn't it - the large scale covers the small area and the small scale covers the large area. That's government!

As a general rule, charts will fall into the following categories:

Sailing Charts - These are the smallest scale charts used for planning, and navigating at sea. The Scale on these charts is generally smaller than 1:600,000.

General Charts - These are for coastwise navigation. Their scales range from about 1:150,000 to 1:600,000.

Coastal Charts - Are intended for inshore coastwise navigation where the course may lie inside some reefs and shoals. The scales run from about 1:50,000 to 1:150,000.

Harbor Charts - For navigating in harbors and small waterways. The scales will be larger than 1:50,000.

Captain Jack's Basic Navigation, By Jack I. Davis

Most charts will also have a *Graphic Scale*, which is a line or bar graph somewhere on the chart, giving distances in nautical miles, yards, statue miles and/or feet and meters. Instead of using these graphic scales you can use the latitude scale on the side of your chart, since one minute (1') of latitude is equal to one nautical mile.

All of the charts we will be dealing with are *Mercature* charts. This type of chart is an attempt to picture the face of the earth, which is round, on a flat surface. This is much like peeling an orange and trying to get the peels to lay flat. It is, however, the best of several methods to picture this impossible situation. Further in your sailing career, you may have need for other types of charts, such as those used in great circle sailing, or polar charts if you decide to sail around one or both poles.

Chart accuracy - Nautical charts go back a long way, and some of the charts we use go back a long way. I currently use charts of central American waters that are British Admiralty charts from surveys of 1884. Yes 1884! You should always use the most recent charts available and these are it.

The surprising thing to me is that these charts are as accurate as they are, which gives you an indication of how sharp some of those old sailors really were. In relation to current technology they are not up to our space age expectations, but they are better than may be expected.

On the other hand, I had talked to a few NOAA (National Oceanic and Atmospheric Administration) employees returning from a re-surveying trip to central America. They found some of the Admiralty charted islands to be as much as three miles in error.

When considering accuracy of charts, we must consider how accurate they were at the start and what changes may have occurred in the meantime. These changes may be sand drifting, shoaling, reef build up, wrecks or changes in aids to navigation.

The man-made changes, such as aids to navigation, are printed regularly in the Local Notice to Mariners. This is published by each Coast Guard Commander for changes within their District. Offshore changes are published by the Defense Mapping Agency (DMA) and are called Notice to Mariners.

When you buy a new chart, it should incorporate all changes to the date of publication. The chart owner/user is responsible for updating the chart with changes that have occurred since the date of publication. Ask your Coast Guard District Aids to Navigation section to place your name on the mailing list to receive Local Notice to Mariners.

You can obtain (at no cost) a chart catalogue at your local chart store, which will show you the various charts available, their scale and the chart number.

Your most important help in chart reading will come from a publication called *Chart No. 1*. This is jointly prepared by the NOAA (National Oceanic and Atmospheric Administration) and the Department of Defense, Defense Mapping Agency. This is a book (not a chart) showing the meaning of all symbols, abbreviations, terms and wavy lines shown on charts. This too is available at most chart stores or from the government book stores.

Chart water depths may have different meanings based on various data. In general, the charted depths are the least favorable, whether it be mean low water data, mean lower low water data, etc. If your chart shows an area with a depth of eight feet, that would be the worst situation. Under normal conditions you may find the depth to be slightly greater.

Chart heights above the water, for clearance under bridges or power lines, is also a worst case situation but is taken from mean high water soundings.

CAUTION: Power line clearances will state Authorized Clearance. Do not test the limits of power cable clearance. The aluminum mast will provide a wonderful conductor making all aboard a wonderful barbecued feast for the fish.

Chapter 10
PLOTTING

To make the work easier, unfold your plotting sheet and scotch tape the corners to a flat work surface. You will also need a good set of parallel rulers and a set of dividers. As you have probably found, a hand held calculator is also valuable in navigation.

Latitude - These lines are circles around the earth, such as the equator. All latitude lines are parallel to each other and are referred to as parallels of latitude.

You could draw circles of latitude anywhere but most charts and globes of the earth show the first circle of latitude 60 nm from the equator, both north and south.

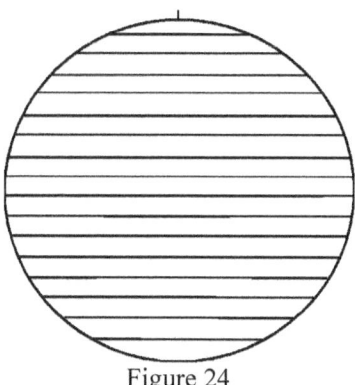
Figure 24

The globe in figure 24 shows parallels of latitude every ten degrees, (600 miles).

This first circle north of the equator is said to be 1' north latitude. Each nautical mile is equal to a minute of latitude, so 90 miles north of the equator is called 1°, 30' north. My boat in the Houston area is 29°, 30' north latitude which means 1770 miles north of the equator. (29.5 x 60 = 1770).

90° north would be a little stake in the snow called the North Pole and is 5,400 miles from the equator.

Next, we need to understand longitude. The longitude lines are half circles around the globe and are not parallel to each other. See figure 25. To draw these circles, you start at one pole and draw a straight line the other pole. The beginning place for numbering these longitude lines is Greenwich, England which is 000° longitude.

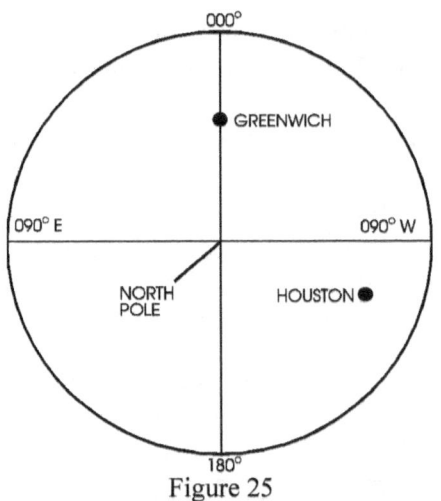

Figure 25

The globe in figure 25 shows a view looking down at the North Pole.

The longitude lines are numbered in a westerly direction from Greenwich, England. They are labeled West, from 000° to 180°. The 180° line is referred to as the International Date Line. As you continue west from the 180° line, the numbers decrease to Greenwich and are labeled East.

Remember: Each minute of latitude, measured vertically, is one mile, but minutes of longitude, measured horizontally, are not equal to one mile (except at the equator), because longitude lines are not parallel.

Figure 26 is an example for locating two geographic points on a chart and measuring the distance between them. The first point is located at 29° 10' North, and 95° 15' West. The second is located at 29° 20' North and 95° 45' West.

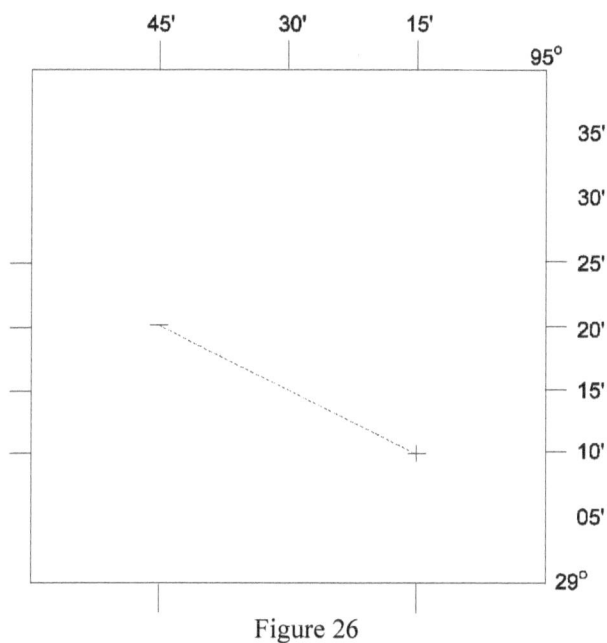

Figure 26

Use the parallel rules across the page for 29° 10' and 95° 15' making a light mark with a sharp pencil. The finer the point, the more accurate the reading. Do the same at 29° 20' North and 95° 45' West. *After the two points are established, determine the distance with dividers, setting one point of the dividers on each point you have marked. Without changing the setting, move the dividers to the vertical scale on the side. Since each minute of latitude is equal to one mile, then twenty-five minutes would be 25 miles.*

Captain Jack's Basic Navigation, By Jack I. Davis

The example in figure 27 shows how to use parallel rules to find the true course from point "A" to point "B." After the course is determined, write it above the line, C 345°. If you have determined your vessel's speed, you will write it below the line.

Never plot anything on your chart except TRUE. There is no place on a chart for a compass course.

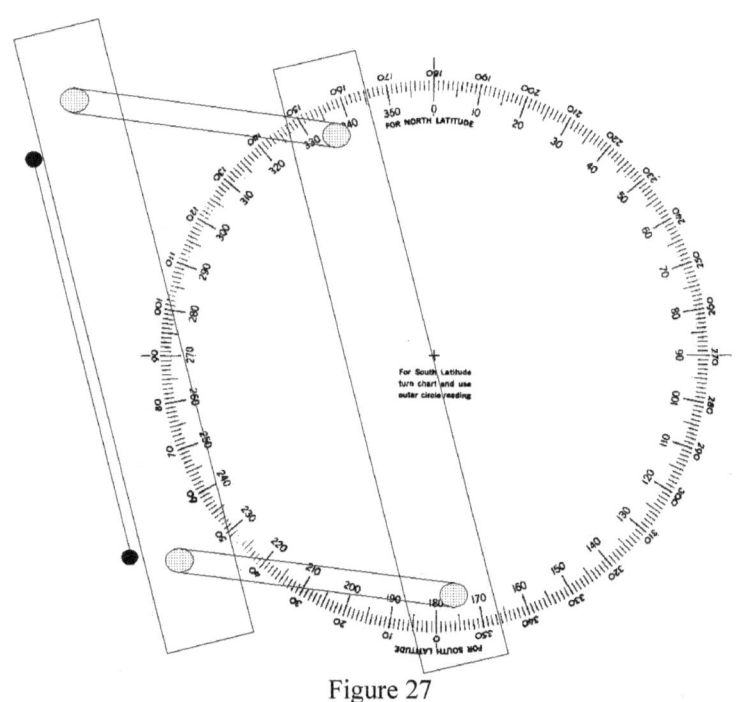

Figure 27

Captain Jack's Basic Navigation, By Jack I. Davis

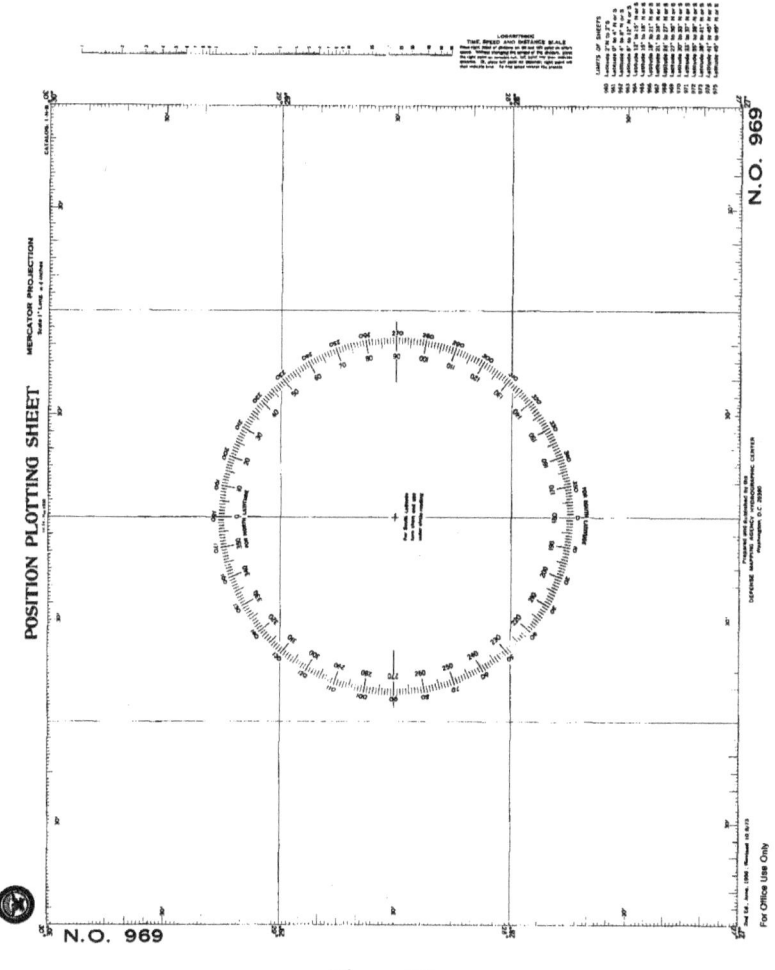

Figure 28

Figure 28 is a very small sample plotting sheet. You can purchase a full scale version (about 16" x 21") at various marine specialty and chart stores. You can have the original copied at any copy or architectural supply center. However, the copies may cost as much as purchasing the plotting sheets.

Below are nine plotting problems. Label the plotting sheet across the top: 97 96 95 94 93 for your longitude lines. The

Captain Jack's Basic Navigation, By Jack I. Davis

latitude lines are already there. Check our solution to these problems at the end of this chapter before continuing on to the stated problems.

    1. Point "A" 27° 10' N, 95° 15' W. Point "B" 27° 50' N, 95° 50' W. With a speed of 6.5 kn what would be:
Time _____? Course _____? Distance _____?

    2. Point "A" 28° 03' N, 95° 58' W. Point "B" 28°57' N, 95° 03' W. With a speed of 4.8 kn what would be:
Time _____? Course _____? Distance _____?

    3. Point "A" 29° 58' N, 95° 55' W. Point "B" 29° 31' N, 95° 11' W. With elapsed time of 8 hr 16 min what is your:
Speed _____? Course _____? Distance _____?

    4. Point "A" 29° 55' N, 94° 17' W. Point "B" 29° 16' N, 94° 54' W. With elapsed time of 7 hr 13 min what is your:
Speed _____? Course _____? Distance _____?

    5. Point "A" 29° 05' N, 94° 45' W. Point "B" 28° 46' N, 93° 56' W. With a speed of 8.3 kn what would be your:
Time _____? Course _____? Distance _____?

    6. Point "A" 28° 28' N, 93° 48' W. Point "B" 29° 03' N, 94° 54' W. With a speed of 9.7 kn what would be your:
Time _____? Course _____? Distance _____?

    7. Point "A" 29° 03' N, 94° 54' W. Point "B" 27° 55' N, 95° 09' W. With elapsed time of 9 hr 56 min what is your:
Speed _____? Course _____? Distance _____?

    8. Point "A" 27° 55' N, 95° 06' W. Point "B" 27° 10' N, 93° 49' W. With elapsed time of 6 hr 42 min what is your:
Speed _____? Course _____? Distance _____?

    9. Point "A" 27° 10' N, 93° 48' W. Point "B" 28° 05' N,

94° 08' W. With elapsed time of 8 hr 59 min what is your:
Speed _____? Course _____? Distance _____?

You will need one or more new plotting sheets to complete the remainder of the questions. Be certain to number the sheet according to the problem you are working.

10. You take three hours to run between marker "A" at 27° 18' N, 91° 50' W, and marker "B" at 27° 37' N, 91° 00' W. The inner compass rose on your chart is affected 011° W and your deviation card indicates a 006° E error. What is your true course _____, compass course _____, magnetic course _____, distance run _____, and speed _____?

11. Point Alpha is located at 29° 00' N and 91° 00' W and bears 275 PSC. Platform Bravo at 29° 10' N and 91° 00' W bears 325 PSC. The chart's inner compass rose indicates a variation of 15° west. The deviation from your deviation card at the time of the sightings was 10° east. There is a current setting SW at 2 knots. After your sighting of Alpha and Bravo, you run two hours on a true course of 045° and then drop anchor. Your speed through the water is 15 knots.

  a. Your position from the two sightings _____? (Fix)

  b. Your estimated position after the two hour run _____?

Label a course line with direction and speed. Above the course line place a capital C followed by three figures to indicate the course steered. The course label should indicate true direction. Below the course line and under the direction label, place a capital S followed by figures representing the speed in knots. Since the course is always given in degrees true and speed in knots, it is not necessary to indicate the units or the reference direction.

Definitions:
Estimated Position - Takes into consideration set and drift, and although it's not a fix it is a major improvement over a DR.
Speed of Advance - The same as speed over the bottom.
Set - The direction the current is going.
Drift - The speed of the current.
Distance Made Good - The geographical distance actually covered.
Speed Made Good - The speed over the bottom.
DR - Your dead reckoning position which takes into consideration only speed through the water and heading.

12. FIRST LEG. You leave your mooring and steer a course of 111° PSC to "C" platform, 17.5 miles distant at 29° 05' N and 89° 30' W. As you cast off, you note a current setting in a westerly direction. Your knot meter indicates 15 knots. Your underway time to "C" platform is 1 hour 16 minutes. Variation in this locality is 12° west. The deviation on this heading is 009° west.

        a. True course to "C" _____?

        b. Drift _____?

        c. Where was your mooring buoy _____?

SECOND LEG. You leave "C" and head for "D" a barge which is located at 29° 59' N and 89° 05' W. It takes five hours to complete this run.

        d. What is your true course _____?

        e. What is your compass course _____?

        f. What is the distance run _____?

g. What is your speed _____?

You must assume the set and drift will remain the same.

13. FIRST LEG. At 1000 you leave your position at 28° 10' N and 89° 55' W steering a course of 081° PSC at 14.5 knots until 1130. Variation in this area is 19° east and deviation is 10° west.

    a. What is your 1130 position _____?

    b. What is your true course _____?

SECOND LEG. At 1130 you change course to 330° true and increase speed to 16 knots. The current is setting NW at 3 knots.

    c. What is your 1530 DR position _____?

    d. What is your 1530 EP _____?

    e. What was your speed of advance from 1130 to 1530 _____?

    f. What was your course made good from 1130 to 1530 _____?

THIRD LEG. At 1530 you change course to 222° true and reduce speed to 15 knots. The set and drift remain the same.

    g. What is your 1700 DR position _____?
    h. What is your 1700 EP _____?

14. FIRST LEG. You depart 28° 30' N, 89° 40' W on a course of 035° PSC at 0900 at a speed of 12 knots. Variation in your locality is 11° east. You calculate the deviation on that

Captain Jack's Basic Navigation, By Jack I. Davis

heading from your deviation table to be 16° west.

    a. Your true course _____?

    b. Your 1300 DR position _____?

SECOND LEG. At 1300. you alter course to 020° true and reduce speed to 10.5 knots. You encounter a current with a westerly set and drift of 4 knots.

    c. Your 1500 DR position _____?

    d. Your 1500 EP _____?

    e. The distance run from 1300 to 1500 _____?

    f. The course made good on this leg _____?

THIRD LEG. At 1500 you change course to 047° PSC and increase speed to 13.3 knots. There is no appreciable current.

    g. Your 1640 DR position _____?

    h. The total distance run from 0900 to 1640 _____?

    i. Your average speed from 0900 to 1640 _____?

15. At 2207 local time, Friday, January 15, you obtain a fix on lighthouse Martha at 27° 00' N, 89° 30' W bearing 132° PSC and drilling rig Kabar bearing 230° PSC. The drilling rigs position is 27° 00' N, 90° 10' W. Variation is 10° west. Your speed is 16 knots and your course is 090° true. The current is setting west at 3 knots. You run until Saturday, January 16 at 007 when you anchor.

    a. Your position at 2207 _____?

b. Your DR position at anchor _____?

c. Your EP at anchor _____?

d. Speed made good _____?

16. FIRST LEG. You depart 1117, production platform "Amigo" at 28° 15' N, 89° 36' W, en route to derrick barge "Bravo" moored next to platform "Charlie" at 28° 36' N, 88° 56' W. You arrive on location at 1517. The variation is 007° W and your deviation is 006° W.

    a. Distance run between Amigo and Charlie _____?

    b. What compass course would you steer _____?

    c. What was your speed from Amigo to Bravo _____?

SECOND LEG. You depart the derrick barge at 1630 on a course of 103° PSC at a speed of 12 knots. At 1700 you sight rig Danny 30° off the port bow. At 1815 rig Danny bears 60° off the port bow.

    d. The true bearing to rig Danny at 1700 _____? and at 1815 _____?

    e. The PSC bearing of rig Danny at 1700 _____? and at 1815 _____?

    f. The position of rig Danny from your two bearings _____?

    g. The distance off Danny at the second bearing _____?

    h. The distance off Danny when abeam _____?

Captain Jack's Basic Navigation, By Jack I. Davis

Captain Jack's Basic Navigation, By Jack I. Davis

PLOTTING ANSWERS

	SPEED	TIME	COURSE	DISTANCE
1.	6.5 kn	7 hr 55 min	$323°$	51.5 nm
2.	4.8 kn	14 hr 35 min	$041.5°$	70 nm
3.	5.75 kn	8 hr 16 min	$124°$	47.5 nm
4.	7.205 kn	7 hr 13 min	$220°$	52 nm
5.	8.3 kn	4 hr 34 min	$115.5°$	38 nm
6.	9.7 kn	7 hr 6.8 min	$302°$	68 nm
7.	6.84 kn	9 hr 56 min	$191°$	68 nm
8.	12.38 kn	6 hr 42 min	$123°$	83 nm
9.	6.456 kn	8 hr 59 min	$341°$	58 nm

10. True course $066°$

  Compass Course $071°$

  Magnetic Course $077°$

  Distance run 47 nm

  Speed 15.66 kn

11. a. 29° 00' N, 90° 50' W

    b. 29° 19' N. 90° 30' W

12. a. 090°

    b. .93 kn

    c. 29° 05' N, 89° 30' W

    d. 035°

    e. 056°

    f. 68 nm

    g. 13.6 kn

13. a. 28° 10' N, 89° 30' W

    b. 090°

    c. 29° 06' N, 90° 05' W

    d. 29° 17' N, 90° 11' W

    e. 19 kn

    f. 330°

    g. 29° 02' N, 90° 27' W

    h. 29° 06' N, 90° 34' W

14. a. 030°

    b. 29° 11.8' N, 89° 13' W

    c. 29° 32' N, 89° 05' W

    d. 29° 32' N, 89° 13.7' W

    e. 19 nm

    f. 358°

    g. 29° 44' N, 89° 00' W

    h. 84 nm

    i. 10.95 kn

15. a. 27° 15' N, 89° 56' W

    b. 27° 15' N, 89° 20' W

    c. 27° 15.3' N, 89° 25' W

    d. 13 kn

16. a. 41.2 nm

    b. 071° PSC

    c. 10.25 kn

    d. 030°, 060°

    e. 043°, 073°

    f. 28° 49' N, 88° 22' W

g. 15 nm

h. 12.5 nm

Chapter 11
FOLLOW YOUR NAVIGATIONAL PLAN

    Years before my sailing life got underway, I took a trip on a Morgan 41 Out Island with an experienced captain on an overnight sail from Miami to Bimini.

    I had never been on a sailboat and had never been out of sight of land. It was a stimulating experience, and in retrospect it was one of the key events that unchained me from a desk.

    Just before dawn the captain left me at the helm so he could get a little sleep. He told me the course to steer, left me with definite instructions not to change course and to call him if there was a problem of any kind.

    After a couple of hours, I spotted a sailboat on the horizon about thirty degrees off to starboard. I concluded he was probably approaching Bimini, probably had it in sight and we were, therefore, off course to the north. I changed course.

    The captain evidently sensed the change and came roaring out on deck immediately to give me the most severe chewing out I have had since I was a teenager. "Don't ever change course unless you are instructed to change course."

    This event made an indelible impression on me and even though over twenty years have gone by, I think of it often. Especially, when I have to leave a novice sailor at the helm.

Captain Jack's Basic Navigation, By Jack I. Davis

I have found there is a strong tendency for sailors to quickly change their plan. This happens when they see something that suggests they are in the wrong place or going in the wrong direction.

Many times students have changed course "because the boat sails better" or "we go much faster on the other course." I have to remind them that sailing better or going faster in the wrong direction accomplishes very little towards their ultimate goal of arriving at a predetermined destination.

On one delivery, I was approaching the Fort Myers Beach outer marker, when one of my crew sang out that the marker was thirty degrees off to port. I was following the GPS heading which was adjusting for a strong current which was setting us north. Our vessel was not pointed at the marker even though we were making good the correct course to the marker.

Other crew joined in, certain we were going in the wrong direction. I ignored them just as I had the first crewman. By following the GPS course we got to within a hundred feet of the marker, at which time the GPS displayed this fact.

I had previously laid out a course of $328°$ to steer after we had the marker abeam. As soon as I turned on that course, my crew spotted a marker thirty degrees off to starboard and concluded, again, that we were going the wrong direction.

I am not saying these things as a put-down of my crew, but more so to emphasize the tendency of many sailors to forget the carefully laid out plan in favor of a haphazard judgment, which may be arrived at during the excitement of the moment.

To sum this up: Have a navigational plan. Be very careful about changing the plan without proper justification. Be very watchful of crew who may try to vary the plan.

Chapter 12
FEAR, REMEMBRANCE AND REALITY

Early in my sailing career, I was sailing my twenty-seven foot Erickson from Galveston to Padre Island (Port Isabel) with a couple of slightly more experienced sailors. Twenty-four hours into the trip or about four o'clock in the afternoon, the wind increased to forty knots and stayed. With the storm sails up I was going along well, but my experienced crew members were getting seasick.

I carried on until midnight, the wind not letting up, possibly increasing slightly and my crew was very sick. I didn't perceive any great danger to the boat, but I was becoming concerned about the crew.

Could people die from seasickness? I didn't know but I was getting worried.

I looked on the chart and found I wasn't far from the entrance to Matagorda Bay. I made a snap decision and changed course. Later, I began thinking about the wind direction and the way the cut into Matagorda Bay was laid out. It became clear the wind would be blowing straight down that cut.

What would the wave conditions be in the cut with this much wind? The charts didn't have that kind of information and

Captain Jack's Basic Navigation, By Jack I. Davis

I didn't know where else to look.

I knew there was a U. S. Coast Guard station on the bay, so I decided to call them on my VHF radio. I would ask them for any information about the storm I was in and see what they knew about the Matagorda cut.

By then I was less than fifteen miles away and they answered immediately. In response to my question about weather conditions, they read the last NOAA report. The same one I had been hearing for the last several hours. "Southeast winds 10 to 15 knots, seas 3 to 5 feet." When I told them I was experiencing light gale conditions, their reply was, "It must be a local disturbance because NOAA said 10 to 15." Of course my local disturbance had been going on for about six hours.

I asked about any possibly dangerous situations that might occur in the Matagorda cut with high winds blowing right down the middle. I said my charts didn't give me any insight into that problem.

Their response was: "You should have all the necessary charts aboard."

Well, so much for local knowledge assistance from the Coast Guard. I thought that if there was a grave and imminent danger, they surely would have told me. I still believe they could have handled this with better than stock answers.

I have been telling the *going-through-the-cut* story for many years: "When I got to the beginning of the channel between the jetties, the following seas changed from fifteen feet to thirty plus feet in a matter of minutes. There was practically no trough between the seas, I would be going down sharply, and then, Bang! I would be going back up. The pressure on the helm was tremendous. I had to brace myself and pull as hard as I could to keep from broaching."

The ups and downs, the pushing and pulling, went on for several hours. By the time I was inside and in smooth water I was absolutely exhausted.

A few years ago, I was back there on a boat delivery in good weather. The length of the cut through the jetties is less than one half mile. The time it would have taken me to get through, even in horrible weather, would have been ten minutes or so.

Looking back on this event, after tens of thousands of sailboat miles at sea and hundreds of real storms, I have had to rethink some of these stories. In the Matagorda cut that night the wind was probably less than forty knots, the seas less than thirty feet and the hours fighting these horrible conditions, were more like minutes.

My fear and exhaustion were real enough, but the rest was an exaggeration. Everything seemed so real, I didn't think I was exaggerating the hundreds of times I told the story.

In several cases where I have had inexperienced crew on boat deliveries, I have heard their stories told. Often the stories were so bizarre I could not believe I was on the same trip. These are good people who are not intentionally exaggerating, it's just the difference in perception of inexperience versus experience. To them the "horrible storm that lasted for hours" was in their minds "a horrible storm that lasted for hours." Whereas I recorded in my log, "We experienced a squall, with winds of thirty knots that lasted ten minutes."

With a green crew, as the wind increases they go through successions of growing fear. As the wind goes from a pleasant 15 knots to 30 knots the wind pressure doubles, the noise doubles and their fear doubles. At 40 knots we have storm sails up and everything has doubled again. At about 55 knots, everything has doubled again. We take down the storm sails and carry on under bare poles. Wind pressure, noise and fear have doubled again at 60 knots and without seeing it you can't believe it. If the wind continues to increase, this doubling effect continues about every 11 knots.

Then another strange thing happens. When the wind drops from 70 knots to 60 knots, it's twice as good as it was. From 60 knots to 50 knots everything is becoming downright pleasant. At 50 knots I have had the green crew come to ask if we can put up sails again. This is the same 50 knots, when the wind was building, where they were so scared they couldn't

Captain Jack's Basic Navigation, By Jack I. Davis

talk.

On one occasion I heard of a story being told by a former crew member about a knockdown we had experienced. I was on the same trip but somehow I missed the knockdown.

A knockdown occurs when the sailboat rolls over with the mast in the water, if not pointing straight down. In my career this has only happened once and it was a freak situation, having to do more with the boat configuration rather than the storm.

The knockdown the crew was talking about was in a situation where we were laying ahull in a storm for twenty-seven hours, and the boat fell on its side three or four times. The mast never got close to going under and the danger to boat and crew was minimal, although the ride was unpleasant.

The crew member really believed he had been in a knockdown. I logged, "Rough seas and an unpleasant ride which interfered with my coffee drinking and gin rummy."

The Matagorda cut situation, even though I misjudged it, can be a very real danger. The problem arises when the water is running out of the bay through the cut and the wind is blowing the opposite direction. This causes the seas to, not only get larger than usual, but also closer together. Through the years I have witnessed this problem at the Galveston Bay inlet, the Penscola Bay inlet, the Gulf Stream around the straits of Florida and up the east coast. When the wind is blowing against the Gulf Stream, the seas become very dangerous. I have described them many times as square waves. My conclusion is to avoid these situations anyway you can because they can do some real damage.

But then you say, "What if I can't avoid it. What if I have to go?" These have been the last words spoken by many sailors and aviators.

You never have to go!!!!! There are always alternatives. The first thing to do is a little book work ahead of time. The *US Coast Pilot* (which I did not have aboard that stormy night) has worlds of information about almost any navigable entrance. In the case of the Matagorda Ship Channel, the *Pilot* shows tidal currents of up to three knots. Another book, *Tidal*

Current Tables gives the times of these tidal changes.

By knowing the outgoing tide could be running three knots and the time of its peak run was the time I happened on the scene, I could have hoved-to off shore for two or three hours and had a smooth run into the bay.

If I could have known how steep the waves were going to be and how hard it would be to control the helm, I would have preferred a few hours of laying ahull.

The Gulf stream is a different problem as it runs up to four knots all the time. The secret is not to be there if heavy winds are blowing against it, which sometimes cannot be predicted.

The saving grace is that almost anywhere along the straits of Florida and up the east coast, you are not far from sanctuary. Many times I have aborted trips across the stream and pulled into a safe anchorage for a few hours to avoid a severe beating.

Now that I've scared everyone with horror stories let me summarize:

1. The wind will not and cannot blow your boat over, it just cannot happen. On a monohull sailing vessel the wind can only push the boat over on its side so far, then there is nothing left for the wind to blow against. The boat will right itself and the process will begin again.

2. Under usual conditions (if there is such a thing), there is a strict consistency in wave height and the distance between wave tops. The more wind velocity, the higher the waves and the further apart they become. In a major storm in the Atlantic, which blew from one direction (north) for several days, the wave heights built to more than fifty feet. However, the distance between the tops was over one-quarter of a mile. I carried on under storm sails through the whole thing and the sailing was not unpleasant.

3. The danger comes when there is tidal movement one way and the wind the opposite. I have had to hove-to in 35 knots of wind in these conditions when the seas were only fifteen feet but they weren't fifty feet apart, and as I said

before, square.

4. If you study the weather broadcast and pick your weather accordingly, you should not have to undergo major trauma on the water. Learning as much as you can about the handling and repair of your boat, along with the proper charts, books, navigational tools, safety gear and back-up gear will give you piece of mind knowing you can handle any situation.

Captain Jack's Basic Navigation, By *Jack I. Davis*

SAILING TERMS SPOKEN EVERY DAY

BITTER END - The last link in a ship's anchor rode and usually attached to the ship by bolt or snap. If you let out all of a ship's anchor rode, you come to the bitter end. The trailing or loose end of a line.

BLAZER - Jacket which derives its name from HMS (Her Majesty's Ship) BLAZER whose captain, in 1845, dressed his crew in special blue and white striped jerseys.

CABOOSE - Housing for the chimney of the cook's galley on a merchant vessel.

CUT AND RUN - To cut through a hemp anchor rode so that the ship can get underway in an emergency. (Or release the bolt from the bitter end.)

DOLDRUMS - Area of low pressure near the equator between the trade winds.

FENDER - Device used to prevent damage by impact, or by chaffing or rubbing.

HIGH AND DRY - Condition of a ship aground so that the tide, falling away, brings her keel above water.

LAID-UP - Said of a vessel when she has been un-rigged and her gear dismantled.

LAND SHARK - Lawyer. Considered to be unlucky to have aboard for any purpose.

LANDMARK - Any distinctive feature ashore, such as a lighthouse, beacon or unusual contour of land, that can serve as an aid to navigation.

LEEWAY - Sideways drift of a vessel to leeward of her course. It was imperative to plot a course that would allow enough leeway to clear a potentially dangerous area.

ON AN EVEN KEEL - Said of a vessel when her keel is horizontal and she draws the same draught of water both forward and aft.

PIPE DOWN - Proper order on early sailing ships to be quiet.

QUEEN OF THE ROAD - A vessel close-hauled and having the right of way.

SCUTTLEBUTT - Lidded cask in which fresh water was kept for daily use. (And where you picked up the latest gossip.)

SON OF A GUN - Derived from the period of time when wives of seamen lived aboard in harbor, (sometimes at sea) and had to give birth between the guns, since the deck gear had to be kept clear.

TAKE A DIFFERENT TACK - A vessel beating to weather changes course from to side to side, is said to be tacking.

TAKEN ABACK - Surprised - Stopped short, as when the wind suddenly changed and back winded your sails, bringing your vessel to a sudden halt.

TOUCH AND GO - To run a vessel aground but float her almost immediately.

UNDERWAY - Not tied to a mooring or to shore.

Captain Jack's Basic Navigation, By Jack I. Davis

SUPPLIERS & MANUFACTURERS

The following list of Suppliers and Manufacturers in no way constitutes a complete directory of all the fine manufacturers and suppliers available throughout the country. This list does not recommend these companies, it should be used only as a reference. As always ask your friends for their recommendations. In most cases you will not be disappointed following their guidance.

SUPPLIERS

Boater's World: Boat Supplies 1-800-826-2628, 6711 Ritz Way, Beltsville, MD   20705
Boat/US: Boat Supplies 1-800-937-2628, 880 S. Pickett St., Alexandria, VA   22304
Defender: Boat Supplies 1-800-628-8225, P. O. Box 820, New Rochelle, NY 10802-0820
E & B Discount Marine: Boat Supplies 1-800-538-0775, P. O. Box 50050, Watsonville, CA 95077-5050
Home Depot: Tools/Supplies Located in most cities throughout the country. Look for them in your local phone books.
Jamestown Distributors: Boat Building/Repairing Supplies 1-800-423-0030, 28 Narragansett Ave., P. O. Box 348

Captain Jack's Basic Navigation, By Jack I. Davis

Jamestown, RI 02835
West Marine: Boat Supplies 1-800-538-0775, P. O. Box 50050, Watsonville, CA 95077-5050

MANUFACTURERS

Ameron Protective Coatings: Coatings, 800-926-3766, 201 North Berry Street, Brea, CA 92621
Apollo Diesel Generators: Gensets, 714-650-2519, 833 West 17th Street #3, Costa Mesa, CA 92627
Balmar: Alternators and Controls, 902 NW Ballard Way, Seattle, WA 98107
Caterpillar Inc.: Engines, 800-321-7332, P. O. Box 610, Mossville, IL 61552
Cummings Southeastern Power Inc.: Engines, 305-821-4200, 9900 NW 77th Court, Hialeah Gardens, FL 33016
Datamarine International Inc.: Electronics Instruments, 508-563-7151, 53 Portside Drive, Pocasset, MA 02559
Davis Instruments: Navigation Instruments, 415-732-9229, 3465 Diablo Ave., Hayward, CA 94545
Detroit Diesel: Engines, 313-592-5000, 7215 South 228th Street, Kent, WA 98032
Espar Heater Systems: Cabin Heaters, 416-670-0960, 6435 Kestrel Road, Mississauga, Ontario, Canada L5T 128
Fireboy Halon Systems Division-Convenience Marine Products, Inc.: Fire Suppression Equipment, 616-454-8337, P O Box 152, Grand Rapids, MI 49501
Furuno USA Inc.: Electronics, 415-873-4421, P. O. Box 2343, South San Francisco, CA 94083
Galley Maid Marine Products, Inc.: Galley, Water Supply and Waste, 407-848-8696, 4348 Westroads Drive, West Palm Beach, FL 33407
Heart Interface Corp.: Inverters, Chargers, Monitors, Electrical, 1-800-446-6180, 21440 68th Ave. South, Kent, WA 98032
Hubbell Wiring Device Division, Hubbell Inc.: Electrical

Products, 203-337-3348, P. O. Box 3999, Bridgeport, CT 06605

Icom America, Inc.: Electronics, 206-454-8155, 2380 - 116th Ave. NE, Bellevue, WA 98004

Indian River Battery: Rebuilt Starters, Alternators, Motors, Batteries, 561-562-3255, 3638 US Hwy. 1, Vero Beach, FL 32960

Interlux Paints: Varnish, Paint, Coatings, 908-964-2285, 2270 Morris Ave., Union, NJ 07083

Kilo Pak: Gensets, 800-824-8256, 190 S Bryan Road, Dania, FL 33004

Kop Coat Marine Coatings: Coatings, 800-221-4466, 36 Pine Street, Rockaway, NJ 07866

Marinco Electrical Products: Electrical Products, 415-883-3347, One Digital Drive, Novato, CA 94949

Mercruiser: Engines, Drives, 800-624-2499, P. O. Box 1226, Waterloo, Iowa 50704

Micrologic: Electronics, 818-998-1216, 20801 Dearborn Street, Chatsworth, CA 91311

Nautical Paint Industries: Coatings, 800-432-4333, 1999 Elizabeth Street, North Brunswick, NJ 08902

New England Ropes, Inc.: All Types of Line, 508-999-2351, Popes Island, New Bedford, MA 02740

Northern Lights: Gensets, P. O. Box 70543, Seattle, WA 98107

Onan: Gensets, 612-574-5000, 1400 73rd Ave. NE, Minneapolis, MN 55432

Paneltronics: Electrical Panels, 305-823-9777, 11960 NW 80th Ct, Hialeah Gardens, FL 33016

Perkins Power Corp.: 305-592-9745, 5820 NW 84th Ave., Miami, FL 33166

Powerline: Alternators and Controls, 1-800-443-9394, 4616 Fairlane Ave., Ft Worth, TX 76119

Racor Division-Parker Hannifin Corporation: Fuel Filters, 800-344-3286, P. O. Box 3208, Modesto, CA 95353

Raritan Engineering Company, Inc.: Heads, Treatment Systems, Charging Systems, 609-825-4900

Ray Jefferson Company: Electronics, 215-487-2800, Main & Cotton Sts., Philadelphia, PA 19127

Raytheon Marine Company: Electronics, 603-881-5200, 46 River Road, Hudson, NH 03051

Resolution Mapping: Electronic Charts and Software 617-860-0430, 35 Hartwell Ave., Lexington, MA 02173

Sea Recovery Corporation: Water Purification, 213-327-4000, P. O. Box 2560, Gardena, CA 90247

Seagull Water Purification Systems: Water purification, 203-384-9335, P O Box 271, Trumbull, CT 06611

Starbrite: Coatings/Sealants 1-305-587-6280, 4041 SW 47th Ave., Ft. Lauderdale, FL 33314

Statpower Technologies Corp: Chargers, Inverters, 7725 Lougheed Hwy, Burnby, BC Canada V5A 4V8

Teak Deck Systems: Teak Deck Caulking 813-377-4100, 6050 Palmer Blvd. Sarasota, FL 34232

The Guest Company, Inc.: Electrical Components, Chargers, Inverters, 203-238-0550, P. O. Box 2059, Station A, Meriden, CT 06450

Trace Engineering: Chargers, Inverters, 206-435-8826, 5917 - 195th NE, Arlington, WA 98223

US Paint: Coatings, 314-621-0525, 831 South 21st Street, Saint Louis, MO 63103

Valspar: Coatings, 612-332-7371, 1101 3rd Street S., Minneapolis, MN 55415

Vanner Weldon Inc. Inverters & Chargers, 614-771-2718, 4282 Reynolds Dr., Hilliard, OH 43026-1297

Webasto Heater, Inc.: Cabin Heaters, 313-545-8770, 1458 East Lincoln, Madison Hts, MI 48071

Westerbeke: Gensets, 508-588-7700, Avon Industrial Park, Avon, MA 02322

West System Epoxy: Gougeon Brothers, Inc., 517-684-7286, P. O. Box 908, Bay City, MI 48707

Woolsey/Z-Spar: Paint, Varnish, Coatings, 800-221-4466, 36 Pine St., Rockaway, NJ 07866

Yanmar: Engines, 800-962-1984, 951 Corporate Grove Drive, Buffalo Grove, IL 60089

Captain Jack's Basic Navigation, By Jack I. Davis

GLOSSARY

This glossary has been compiled through a joint effort of the staff of Bristol Fashion Publications and many writers. It is not intended to cover the many thousands of words and terms contained in the language exclusive to boating. The longer you are around boats and boaters the more of this second language you will learn.

A

Accumulator tank-A tank used to add air pressure to the fresh water system thus reducing water pump run time.
Aft-Near the stern.
Amidships-Midway between the bow and stern.
Antifouling-Bottom paint used to prevent growth on the bottom of boats.
Arrangement Plan-The drawing that shows the berths, galley and head inside the hull.
Athwartships-Any line running at a right angle to the fore/aft centerline of the boat.

B

Backer plate-Metal plate used to increase the strength of a through bolt application, such as with the installation of a cleat.
Ballast-Weight added to improve sea handling abilities of the boat or to counter balance an unevenly loaded boat.

Beam-The width of the boat at it's widest point.
Bilge-The lowest point inside a boat.
Bilge pump-Underwater water pump used to remove water from the bilge.
Binnacle-A box or stand used to hold the compass.
Body Plan-The drawing showing the shape of the hull in an athwartships plane. Also called Sections.
Bolt-Any fastener with any head style and machine thread shank.
Boot stripe-Trim paint of a contrasting color located just above the bottom paint on the hull sides.
Breaker-Replaces a fuse to interrupt power on a given electrical circuit when that circuit becomes overloaded or shorted.
Bridge-The steering station of a boat.
Brightwork-Polished metal or varnished wood aboard a boat.
Bristol Fashion-The highest standard of condition any vessel can obtain and the highest state of crew seamanship. The publishing company which brought you this book.
Bulkhead-A wall running across (athwartships) the boat.
Butt connectors-A type of crimp connector used to join two wires end to end in a continuing run of the wire.

C

Canvas-A general term used to describe cloth material used for boat coverings of any type. A type of cloth material.
Carlin-A structural beam joining the inboard ends of deck beams that are cut short around a mast or hatch.
Cavitation-Reduced propeller efficiency due to vapor pockets in areas of low pressure on the blades. Turbulence caused by prop rotation which reduces the efficiency of the prop.
Center of Effort-(CE) The geometric center of the total sail plan on a sailboat. Used to determine lee or weather helm.
Center of Lateral Plane-The geometric center of the (CLP)

underwater profile on sailboats used with CE, above.

Centerboard-A hinged board or plate at the bottom of a sailboat of shallow draft. It reduces leeway under sail.

Chafing gear-Any material used to prevent the abrasion of another material.

Chain locker-A forward area of the vessel used for chain storage.

Chain-Equally sized inter-looping oblong rings commonly used for anchor rode.

Chine-The intersection of the hull side with the hull bottom, usually in a moderate speed to fast hull. Sailboats and displacement speed powerboats usually have a round bilge and do not have a chine. Also, the turn of the hull below the waterline on each side of the boat. A sailboat hull, displacement hull and semi-displacement hull all have a round chine. Planing hulls all have a hard (sharp corner) chine.

Chock-A metal fitting used in mooring or rigging to control the turn of the lines.

Cleat-A device used to secure a line aboard a vessel or on a dock.

Clevis-A "Y" shaped piece of sailboat hardware about two to four inches long that connects a wire rope rigging terminal to one end of a turnbuckle.

Coaming-A barrier around the cockpit of a vessel to prevent water from washing into the cockpit.

Cockpit-Usually refers to the steering area of a sailboat or the fishing area of a sport fishing boat. The sole of this area is always lower than the deck.

Companionway-An entrance into a boat or a stairway from one level of a boat's interior to another.

Construction Plan-A drawing showing all the parts that make up the hull structure. The plan and profile are drawn.

Cribbing-Large blocks of wood used to support the boat's hull during it's time on land.

Cutless Bearing®-A rubber tube that is sized to a propeller shaft and which fits inside the propeller shaft strut.

D

Davit-Generally used to describe a lifting device for a dinghy.

Deadrise-The angle that a hull bottom makes with the horizontal. Measured in the aft part of the hull but more commonly at the stern. If the stern is flat from port to starboard, it has zero deadrise.

Deck Plan-A drawing showing all the structure and hardware on the deck.

Deck Camber-An arbitrary curve that the deck has from port to starboard.

Delaminate-A term used to describe two or more layers of any adhered material that have separated from each other due to moisture or air pockets in the laminate.

Device-A term used in conjunction with electrical systems. Generally used to describe lights, switches, receptacles, etc.

Dinghy-Small boat used as a tender to the mother ship.

Displacement-The amount of water, in weight, displaced by the boat when floating.

Displacement Hull - A hull that has a wave crest at bow and stern and which settles in the wave trough in the middle. A boat supported by its own ability to float while underway.

Dock-Any land-based structure used for mooring a boat.

Down Flooding-When water enters an open hatch or ladder.

Draft-The distance from the waterline to the keel bottom. The amount of space (water) a boat needs between its waterline and the bottom of the body of water. When a boat's draft is greater than the water depth, you are aground.

Dry rot-This is not a true term as the decay of wood actually occurs in moist conditions.

F

Fairing-The process of smoothing a portion of the boat so it will present a very even and smooth surface after the finish is applied.

Fairing compound-The material used to achieve the fairing process.

Fairlead-A portion of rigging used to turn a line, cable or chain to increase the radius of the turn and thereby reduce friction.

Fall-The portion of a block and tackle system that moves up or down.

Fastening-Generally used to describe a means by which the planking is attached to the structure of the boat. Also used to describe screws, rivets, bolts, nails, etc. (fastener)

Fiberglass-Cloth-like material made from glass fibers and used with resin and hardener to increase the resin strength.

Filter-Any device used to filter impurities from any liquid or air.

Fin keel-A recent type of keel design. Resembles an up-side-down T when viewed from fore or aft.

Flame arrestor-A safety device placed on top of a gasoline carburetor to stop the flame flash of a backfiring engine.

Flat head-A screw head style which can be made flush with or recessed into the wood surface.

Float switch-An electrical switch commonly used to automatically control the on-off of a bilge pump. When this device is used, the pump is considered to be an automatic bilge pump.

Flying bridge-A steering station high above the deck level of the boat.

Fore-The front of a boat.

Fore-and-aft-A line running parallel to the keel. The keel runs fore-and-aft.

Forecastle-The area below decks in the forward most section of the boat. (pronunciation is often fo'c's'le)

Foredeck-The front deck of a boat.

Forward-Any position in front of amidships.

Freeboard-The distance on the hull from the waterline to the deck level.
Full keel-A keel design with heavy lead ballast and deep draft. This keel runs from the stem, to the stern at the rudder.

G

Galley-The kitchen of a boat.
Gelcoat-A hard, shiny coat over a fiberglass laminate which keeps water from the structural laminate.
Gimbals-A method of supporting anything which must remain level regardless of the boat's attitude.
Grommet-A ring pressed into a piece of cloth through which a line can be run.
Gross tonnage-The total interior space of a boat.
Ground tackle-Refers to the anchor, chain, line and connections as one unit.

H

Hanging locker-A closet with a rod for hanging clothes.
Hatch-An opening with a lid which opens in an upward direction.
Hauling-Removing the boat from the water. The act of pulling on a line or rode is also called hauling.
Hawsehole-A hull opening for mooring lines or anchor rodes.
Hawsepipes-A pipe through the hull, for mooring or anchor rodes.
Head-The toilet on a boat. Also refers to the entire area of the bathroom on a boat.
Helm-The steering station and steering gear.
Holding tank-Used to hold waste for disposal ashore.
Hose-Any flexible tube capable of carrying a liquid.
Hull-The structure of a vessel not including any component other than the shell.
Hull lines-The drawing of the hull shape in plan, profile and sections (body plan).

I

Inboard-Positioned towards the center of the boat. An engine mounted inside the boat.

Inboard Profile-A drawing of the centerline profile of a boat showing the interior arrangement on one side.

K

Keel-A downward protrusion running fore and aft on the center line of any boat's bottom. It is the main structural member of a boat.

King plank-The plank on the center line of a wooden laid deck.

Knees-A structural member reinforcing and connecting two other structural members. Also, two or more vertical beams at the bow of a tugboat used to push barges.

L

Launch-To put a boat in the water.

Lazarette-A storage compartment in the stern of a boat.

Lead-The material used for ballast. Also, pronounced "leed", (as in leading a horse) when denoting the distance separating CE and CLP in a sail plan (See above).

Limber holes-Holes in the bilge timbers of a boat to allow water to run to the lowest part of the bilge where it can be pumped out.

LOA-Length Over All. The overall length of a boat.

Locker-A storage area.

Log-A tube or cylinder through which a shaft or rudder stock runs from the inside of the boat to the outside of the boat. The log will have a packing gland (stuffing box) on the inside of the boat. Speed log is used to measure distance traveled. A book used to keep record of the events on board a boat.

LWL-Length On The Waterline. The length of a boat at the waterline.

M

Manifold-A group of valves connected by piping to tanks. They allow filling and removal from one or more tanks.

Marine gear-The term used for a boat's transmission.

Mast-An upward pointing timber used as the sail's main support. Also used on power and sailboats to mount flags, antennas and lights.

Metacenter-A graphically determined point in stability calculations at one angle of heel.

Mile-A statute mile (land mile) is 5280 feet. A nautical mile (water mile) or knot is 6080.2 feet.

Mizzen mast-The aftermost mast on a sailboat.

Mold loft-A floor where hull lines are drawn full size. Patterns for construction are taken from the mold loft.

Moment-A force (pounds) multiplied by the length of a lever arm (inches) to where the force is applied. (lb-in) If this is a rotating force on a shaft it is called torque or torsion. (lb-in). Bending Moment is the force applied to a plate or beam which tends to bend the beam or plate.

Moment of Inertia-Expressed as 'I' in the units (inches^4). Indicates the resistance to motion (stiffness) of a particular structural shape.

N

Nautical mile-A distance of 6080.2 feet

Navigation lights-Lights required to be in operation while underway at night. The lighting pattern varies with the type, size and use of the vessel.

Nut-A threaded six sided device used in conjunction with a bolt.

Nylon-A material used for lines when some give is desirable. Hard nylon is used for some plumbing and rigging fittings.

O

Outboard Profile-A drawing of the outside of a hull. Sometimes called a styling drawing.

Oval head-A screw head design used when the head can only be partially recessed. The raised (oval) portion of the head will remain above the surface.

Overhangs-The length from the bow or stern ending of the waterline to the forward or aft end of the hull.

P

Painter-A line used to tow or secure a small boat or dinghy.

Pan head-A screw head design with a flat surface, used when the head will remain completely above the surface.

Panel-A term used to describe the main electrical distribution point, usually containing the breakers or fuses.

Pier-Same general usage as a dock.

Pile-A concrete or wooden post driven or otherwise embedded into the water's bottom.

Piling-A multiple structure of piles.

Pipe-A rigid, thick walled tube.

Planing hull-A hull design, which under sufficient speed, will rise above it's dead in the water position and seem to ride on the water.

Planking-The covering members of a wooden structure.

Plug-A term used to describe a pipe, tubing or hose fitting. Describes any device used to stop water from entering the boat through the hull. A cylindrical piece of wood placed in a screw hole to "hide" the head of the screw.

Port-A land area for landing a boat. The left side of the boat when facing forward.

Prismatic Coefficient- (Cp) A dimensionless ratio of the hull displacement in cubic feet divided by the product of waterline length multiplied by area of the largest submerged hull section.

Propeller-Located at the end of the shaft. The prop must have at least two blades and propels the vessel through the water with a screwing motion. (Prop, Wheel, Screw)

R

Radar-A electronic instrument which can be used to see objects as blips on a display screen.

Rahola Criteria-Named after the person who proposed this measure of boat stability. Using a curve of Righting Arms at various angles of heel, the area under the curve to 40 degrees of heel must be 15 ft-degrees.

Rail-A non-structural safety member on deck used as a banister to help prevent falling overboard.

Reduction gear-The gear inside the transmission housing that reduces the engine Rpm to a propeller shaft Rpm that is optimum for that particular hull and engine.

Ribs-Another term for frames. The planking is fastened to these structural members.

Rigging-Generally refers to any item placed on the boat after the delivery of the vessel from the manufacturer. Also refers to all the wire rope, line, blocks, falls and other hardware needed for sail control.

Righting Arm-A term used in stability calculations. The distance between the center of gravity of a hull and the center of buoyancy at one particular angle of heel.

Ring terminals-A crimp connector with a ring which can have a screw placed inside the ring for a secure connection.

Rode-Anchor line or chain.

Rope-Is a term which refers to cordage and this term is only used on land. When any piece of cordage is on board a boat, it is referred to as line or one of it's more designating descriptions.

Round head-A screw or bolt head design with a round surface which remains completely above the material being fastened.

Rudder-Located directly behind the prop and is used to control the steering of the boat.

Rudder stock-Also known as rudder post. A piece of round, solid metal attached to the rudder at one end and the steering quadrant at the other.

S

Samson post-A large piece of material extending from the keel upward through the deck and is used to secure lines for mooring or anchoring.

Screw-A threaded fastener. A term for propeller.

Screw thread-A loosely spaced course thread used for wood and sheet metal screws.

Sea cock-A valve used to control the flow of water from the sea to the device it is supplying.

Section Modulus-Expressed as SM in the units (inches^3). Used in some formulas in place of "I", above. Indicates the resistance to motion (stiffness) of a structural shape.

Sections-Also, Body Plan. The shape of a hull in an athwartships plane, that is perpendicular to the waterline.

Shackle-A metal link with a pin to close the opening. Commonly used to secure the anchor to the rode.

Shaft-A solid metal cylinder which runs from the marine gear to the prop. The prop is mounted on the end of the shaft.

Shear Pin-A small metal pin which is inserted through the shaft and the propeller on small boats. If the prop hits a hard object the shear pin will shear without causing severe damage to the shaft.

Sheaves-The rolling wheel in a pulley.

Sheet metal screw-Any fastener which has a fully threaded shank of wood screw threads.

Ship-Any seagoing vessel. To ship an item on a boat means to bring it aboard.

Shock cord-An elastic line used to dampen the shock stress of a load.

Slip-A docking space for a boat. A berth.

Sole-The cabin and cockpit floor.
Spade Rudder-A rudder that is not supported at its bottom.
Stability-The ability of a hull to return to level trim after being heeled by the forces of wind or water.
Stanchion-A metal post which holds the lifelines or railing along the deck's edge.
Starboard-The right side of the boat when facing forward.
Statute Mile-A land mile which is 5280 feet.
Stem-The forward most structural member of the hull.
Step-The base of the mast where the mast is let into the keel or mounted on the keel in a plate assembly.
Stern-The back of the boat.
Strut-A metal supporting device for the shaft.
Stuffing box-The interior end of the log where packing is inserted to prevent water intrusion from the shaft or rudder stock.
Surveyor-A person who inspects the boat for integrity and safety.
Switch-Any device, except breakers, which interrupt the flow of electrical current to a usage device.

T

Table of Offsets-The collection of measurements taken from the hull lines at each section (or station). Used to draw the hull lines full size on the mold loft floor. It shows the waterlines, butts, sheer and chine in width and height.
Tachometer-An instrument used to count the revolutions of anything turning, usually the engine, marine gear or shaft.
Tack rag-A rag with a sticky surface used to remove dust before applying a finish to any surface.
Tank-Any container of size that holds a liquid.
Tapered Plug-A wooden dowel tapered to a blunt point that is inserted into a seacock or hole in the hull in an emergency.

Tender-A term used to describe a small boat (dinghy) used to travel between shore and the mother ship.
Terminal Lugs-Car-style battery cable ends.
Through hull-Any fitting between the sea and the boat which goes through the hull material. (Thru hull)
Tinned wire-Stranded copper wire with a tin additive to prevent corrosion.
Topsides-Refers to being on deck. The part of the boat above the waterline.
Torque (or Torsion)-The rotating force on a shaft (lb-in).
Transmission-Refers to a marine or reduction gear.
Transom-The flat part of the stern.
Trim-The attitude with which the vessel floats or moves through the water.
Trip line-A small line made fast to the crown of the anchor. When weighing anchor this line is pulled to back the anchor out and thus release the anchor's hold in the bottom.
Tubing-A thin walled cylinder of metal or plastic, similar to pipe but having thinner walls.
Turn of the bilge-A term used to refer to the corner of the hull where the vertical hull sides meet the horizontal hull bottom.
Turnbuckles-In England they are called bottle screws. They secure the wire rope rigging to the hull and are used to adjust the tension in the wire rope.

V

Valves-Any device which controls the flow of a liquid.
Vessel-A boat or ship.
VHF Radio-The electronic radio used for short range (10 to 20 mile maximum range) communications between shore and vessels, and between vessels.

W

Wake-The movement of water as a result of a vessel's movement through the water.

Washer-A flat circular piece of metal with a hole in the center. A washer is used to increase the holding power of a bolt and nut by distributing the stress over a larger area.

Waste pump-Any device used to pump waste.

Water pump-Any device used to pump water.

Waterline-The line created at the intersection of the vessel's hull and the water's surface. A horizontal plane through a hull that defines the shape on the hull lines. The actual waterline or just waterline, is the height at which the boat floats. If weight is added to the boat, it floats at a deeper waterline.

Web Frame-The transverse structural members (frames) in a boat hull, installed port to starboard. Longitudinal frames are installed fore and aft.

Weight list-A compilation of every item in the boat. A calculation is made of the weight and center of gravity of everything on board. This is the only way a designer can estimate the displacement of the boat.

Wheel-Another term for prop or the steering wheel of the boat.

Whipping-Refers to any method used, except a knot, to prevent a line end from unraveling.

Winch-A device used to pull in or let out line or rode. It is used to decrease the physical exertion needed to do the same task by hand.

Windlass-A type of winch used strictly with anchor rode.

Woodscrew-A fastener with only two thirds of the shank threaded with a screw thread.

Y

Yacht-A term used to describe a pleasure boat of some size. Usually used to impress someone.

Yard-A place where boats are stored and repaired.

Z

Zebra Mussel-A small fresh water mussel which will clog anything in a short period of time.

Books published by Bristol Fashion Publications
Free catalog, phone 1-800-478-7147
www.bfpbooks.com

Boat Repair Made Easy — Haul Out
Written By John P. Kaufman

Boat Repair Made Easy — Finishes
Written By John P. Kaufman

Boat Repair Made Easy — Systems
Written By John P. Kaufman

Boat Repair Made Easy — Engines
Written By John P. Kaufman

Standard Ship's Log
Designed By John P. Kaufman

Large Ship's Log
Designed By John P. Kaufman

Designing Power & Sail
Written By Arthur Edmunds

Building A Fiberglass Boat
Written By Arthur Edmunds

Buying A Great Boat
Written By Arthur Edmunds

Boater's Book of Nautical Terms
Written By David S. Yetman

Practical Seamanship
Written By David S. Yetman

Captain Jack's Basic Navigation
Written By Jack I. Davis

Creating Comfort Afloat
Written By Janet Groene

Living Aboard
Written By Janet Groene

Racing The Ice To Cape Horn
Written By Frank Guernsey & Cy Zoerner

Marine Weather Forecasting
Written By J. Frank Brumbaugh

Complete Guide To Gasoline Marine Engines
Written By John Fleming

Complete Guide To Outboard Engines
Written By John Fleming

Complete Guide To Diesel Marine Engines
Written By John Fleming

Trouble Shooting Gasoline Marine Engines
Written By John Fleming

Trailer Boats
Written By Alex Zidock

Skipper's Handbook
Written By Robert S. Grossman

White Squall
The Last Voyage Of Albatross
Written By Richard E. Langford

Cruising South
What to Expect Along The ICW
Written By Joan Healy

Electronics Aboard
Written By Stephen Fishman

Five Against The Sea
A True Story of Courage & Survival
Written By Ron Arias

Scuttlebutt
Seafaring History & Lore
Written By Captain John Guest USCG Ret.

Cruising The South Pacific
Written By Douglas Austin

Catch of The Day
Catch It * Clean It * Cook It
Written By Carla Johnson

VHF Marine Radio Handbook
Written By Mike Whitehead

Captain Jack's Basic Navigation, By Jack I. Davis

ABOUT THE AUTHOR

Captain Jack I. Davis and his first mate Mary (Mary is an excellent sailor and registered nurse) have lived aboard their forty-three foot Wauquiez ketch since 1984.

His first career was banking and his second career was computer software for banks but his main love has always been sailboats. During this time he owned several power boats and enjoyed water skiing and fishing but yearned for the blue water which the Texas lakes did not offer.

He had made several ocean crossings before obtaining his first U. S. Coast Guard Captain's License in 1984 at which time he started boat deliveries in earnest.

The majority of the deliveries have been from Texas to Florida and the West Indies with one delivery completely circumnavigating the Gulf of Mexico. In May 1998, he made his sixty-first open water crossing of the Gulf of Mexico.

Between deliveries he has taught countless sailing and navigation classes. His sense of humor and teaching style, as demonstrated in this book, keep his students coming back for more.

He has continually upgraded that first license and now holds a U. S. Coast Guard Master's License, Steam, MotorSail and Sail.

www.ingramcontent.com/pod-product-compliance
Lightning Source LLC
Chambersburg PA
CBHW020358170426
43200CB00005B/213